SIMPLE
HAPPY
PARENTING

This book is dedicated to my own parents,
Roxanne and Arnie—who endured nearly two decades
of my very messy room and taught me more about
life than I could have ever learned from a book.

SIMPLE HAPPY PARENTING

The secret of less for calmer parents and happier kids

Denaye Barahona Ph.D.

WHITE LION PUBLISHING

CONTENTS

INTRODUCTION
WELCOME TO A SIMPLER WAY

LETTER TO THE READER

Dear friends,

Like most parents, I had the best of intentions.

When I was pregnant with my first child, I knew one thing for sure. I knew I wanted to give my children the world. Every generation naturally wants to give their children more than they had themselves. I intended to give my children more.

More love. More protection. More toys. More opportunities.

More, more, and more. I wanted to do everything and be everything for my family. During my first pregnancy, this desire for more was rooted in love.

But after the birth of my first child I felt a dramatic shift. The desire quickly became rooted in fear—and sometimes fear and love can mesh together in ways that are impossible to pick apart. I found myself wondering, if I didn't play with them enough, would they be happy? If I didn't stand at least two feet from them at all times on the playground, would they fall? If I didn't feed them organic food, would their brains be impacted?

All this fear (camouflaged as love) quickly started to take a toll on me. Trying to be everything and do everything for my children left me depleted. My desire to give my children **more** left me feeling *less*.

Less energy. Less joy. Less calm.

Families of today have busy, hurried, noisy lives. I know this in my personal life, but also in my professional life. I have a Ph.D. in Child Development with a specialty in Family Wellness. I work with families to find quiet amidst the noise. This work is worthy and the goals are tangible—you can absolutely find simplicity and happiness for your family too.

This book is the story of finding simplicity for my own family. Invariably, your story will look different. But it will be equally beautiful and important. I will caution you—because I know you have the best of intentions, too. Do not read this book with a list of boxes to check off and a lifestyle to emulate. *You are too extraordinary for that.* You will never fit into any perfectly shaped box or any expert-defined parenting philosophy.

Instead, I hope that you find hope and inspiration amidst the words in this book. Use it as a support tool on your journey, but don't make it your Bible. I believe this book will resonate with you and you will take away many important tools, but I also invite you to leave whatever doesn't suit you and your family. I want to help you seek out simplicity and happiness, but also empower you to write your own story. One that is perfectly made for you.

Warmly (with the best of intentions),

PS: If you are reading this and find yourself wanting to learn more, join the Simple Families Community and one of our online programs.

WHAT IS SIMPLE PARENTING?

Monday morning came too quickly. The weekend had left me feeling unrefreshed. We attended two birthday parties, made a trip to the zoo, and caught up on errands—weekends these days felt like a race against time. Amidst the busyness, I had too many glasses of Pinot Noir to take the edge off a long week of balancing motherhood and life. All this landed me in my current position: at Starbucks in need of a quick fix.

I juggled an oversized infant carseat with an oversized infant inside, attempting to not bump into one of the many tired folks standing in line next to me. As I scanned the coffee shop I quickly locked eyes with my fellow-mom friend, Eden.

Eden was sporting the same oversized infant accessories and tired eyes.

"Hi friend, how was your weekend," she asked me.

I responded in familiar fashion, "Busy. I'm exhausted."

"Yeah, I hear you. I already need a nap," she related.

Eden and I had met at a baby playdate and connected quickly. She was calm, smart, and had a messy house that rivaled mine. We were merely nine months into motherhood and already immersed into the harried culture of "busy" that pervades families of today.

We grew closer as our infants grew into toddlers. Her daughter started to walk, and my son didn't. Months went by as I waited anxiously for him to get closer to this big milestone.

I coped with my anxiety by *doing* everything a mother could do.

I bought him all the stuff. The stuff included three different types of baby-walkers and five pairs of shoes (hard-soled, soft-soled, high-tops, low-tops, *and* leather moccasins).

I scheduled all the appointments. I took him to six different professionals: two pediatricians, a physical therapist, two occupational therapists, and a podiatrist. All of whom silently rolled their eyes at my crazy and sent me away with the suggestion to "give him more time."

So I went to Eden. I asked her a poignant question.

"Do you ever worry about worrying too much?" I wondered out loud.

I can't recall how she answered. However, it didn't matter, because when I heard my question aloud I heard all of the answers I needed.

As a new mother, I realized I was blinded by the amount of fear that is hidden in love. I was blinded by the fact that good intentions can manifest themselves as pressure, stress, overwhelm, and the accumulation of stuff.

My son walked, albeit late. And on the day he walked, I didn't allow myself to relish in that milestone. Instead, my brain kept chugging along.

"Okay, now when will he jump?"

But I caught myself in that thought. I caught myself racing through life and throwing my first-born child into that wretched race as well.

That was the day that I said "no more." I decided that it no longer mattered when he walked, jumped, or read his first book.

I pulled myself, my baby, and our future as a family out of the race.

Parenting in today's world is heavy. Family life is cluttered with an abundance of "must-dos" and "must-haves." We feel the push to do more, have more, work more, and accomplish more. And somewhere along the way, children have become a personal measuring stick for our own success.

That measuring stick is accessible to the public in the form of social media. How many likes did the clip of your daughter's ballet performance receive? Did your son pull more As than your friend's son this semester?

This measuring stick and cluttered family life come at a significant cost: *the well-being of our children.*

As parents, we mostly have the same goals. We strive to raise children that are happy, healthy, and successful.

Yet, there is so much irony in the way we set out to achieve those goals. We want to do it all and be it all for our children, but in the process we end up overparenting. When we overparent, we attempt to manage the intricate details of our children's lives. Cluttered family life occurs when we make significant efforts to protect our children from everyday physical and emotional distress and end up *all sorts of stressed out as a result.*

Watching children experience hurt and failure is excruciating for parents. We will go to great lengths to protect ourselves from that pain. Therefore we carry bags of snacks to prevent hunger. We equip our furniture with padding to prevent bumps and bruises. We sign our kids up for extra soccer camps to "get a leg up." We buy them favored toys and gadgets to see more smiles and prevent envy. We do, do, do. More, more, more.

So what's the verdict? Does overparenting lead to happy, healthy, and successful children?

Not exactly. Let's break down those goals:

HAPPY

Overparenting leads to…no surprise here: **overwhelm**. When we buy everything and do everything, we do not end up with happier kids. In fact, research shows children play better when they have *fewer* toys. And they become more independent when we let them do things for themselves. So what does overparenting lead us to?

Burn out.

Children are mirrors and reflect the feelings and emotions of their parents. And due to the fact that the parents of today are stressed and overwhelmed, the children of today are also stressed and overwhelmed.

Sometimes we think we can hide these emotions from our kids. But alas, we cannot. Those intuitive little people can read us like picture books. Science tells us that our offspring can sense our feelings and frustrations from the earliest months of their lives—it's called social referencing and starts in infancy.

The result is that stress and anxiety are an epidemic in childhood. When family life is infiltrated with high levels of stress, clutter, and overwhelm it will impact the emotional wellbeing of the adults and children alike. Rearing our children in a stressed out, cluttered family environment may put them at risk for mental health challenges both in the present and in the future.

HEALTHY

The health and development of overwhelmed children is at risk. High levels of stress in childhood are related to numerous physical health consequences and chronic disease later in life.

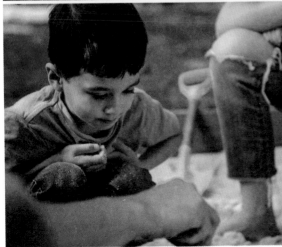

The long-term health risks are clear, but busyness also has a direct impact on the nutritional intake of our families. We know that highly scheduled families rarely eat meals together at home and as a result eat a poorer quality of diet. When you are rushing from soccer to ballet to band practice, you probably aren't doing much home-cooking.

Children who are busy all the time also play less and sleep less. You might be thinking they get lots of activity at baseball practice, right? Actually, there is growing evidence that indicates kids get significantly less exercise in structured activities as opposed to free, unstructured play. Yet we know that free play in childhood is on the decline with busyness being one of the leading causes.

These children are also sleeping less. We know that sleep is vital to the overall well-being and development of children. A growing child requires significant amounts of sleep on a daily basis. Yet the rising number of commitments and obligations that are present in family life today lead to a decline in the quantity and quality of sleep in childhood.

SUCCESSFUL

We want our children to be successful in school and future careers. The result is that often parents push children into academics and school work that they aren't quite ready to complete. Studies show that children who start academic work too young struggle to focus and have higher rates of ADHD.

This phenomenon is present throughout childhood. The importance of play is discounted. Children are pushed to learn the ABCs and 123s before their young brains are ready. There are even apps designed for infants to teach them these pre-academic skills. The result? *Those kids push back.* They fail to fall in love with learning in the way that they should in the early years. This may lead to resistance and struggle as they enter into more formal schooling.

But what if we just did as all those professionals directed me in my early days of parenting?

What if we could just give them the gift of more time?

Not only does pressure and stress impact success, but clutter does as well. We know that children have more difficulty focusing and learning in environments that are physically cluttered. Clutter and distractions prevent children from focusing and are associated with decreased test scores in a classroom setting. Depression, anxiety, and low self-esteem are associated with stress and may prevent children from reaching their full potential in school and in future careers.

But wait a minute? Didn't we say we wanted our kids to be healthy, happy, and successful?

How did we stray so far from these well-intentioned goals? How do we get back to them?

The answer: *Simple Happy Parenting.*

LESS EXPECTATION: LETTING GO OF PERFECT

I want to introduce you to June. She is the perfect mom. June is a mother of four children. She starts each day before the sun comes up with an hour of yoga, meditation, and journaling. June is a stay-at-home-mother who lives every day with a sense of calm and a smile on her face. She strikes a balance between family and career, as she works from home as the CEO of a successful business. She loves her work and has found great success in that part of her life.

June keeps a flawless home and always has freshly baked cookies ready for any surprise visitors (whom she welcomes with open arms into her perfectly tidy home). She takes regular weekends away with both her husband and girlfriends—all of whom she maintains a positive and warm relationship with.

June's job keeps her connected to the world. She frequently has business meetings and phone calls during the day. Fortunately, her children play independently for hours on end so that they do not disrupt her while she is working.

She reads dozens of books to each child during the daytime as it is important to give them individual attention. But she also leads them in collaborative activities, like growing organic food on their own small sustainable backyard farm.

June's children are very well-behaved. They sit quietly during meals in restaurants and clean their plates. But they also know how to let loose and have a lot of fun at all the right moments (as does June). All four children sleep through the night, eat their vegetables, and are completely potty-trained (even the baby).

June sounds pretty fabulous, right? Do you want to know all of her secrets?

June is fiction. This woman does not exist on Earth. The perfect ideals that she represents are unrealistic. Yet, across the world, women find themselves striving for the life that she lives: a perfect, flawless, balanced life.

If June was a human, she should probably be writing this book. But since she isn't available, I am writing it instead. And as an actual human mother, I want to tell you that you need to give yourself the permission to be a real, flawed human being.

I invite you to be a mother who cries, gets upset, and throws a frozen pizza in the oven on the tough days. Be a real-life mother who has imperfect children. Because someone will always pee the bed. Someone else will always toss the vegetables on the floor. And it is unlikely that you will be able to take a phone call without interruption for at least twenty more years.

Do your absolute best job as a mother, but let go of June. If you strive to be her, you will fall short for the rest of your days. Instead of chasing the impossible, choose to live simply and love immensely. Be the best *you* that you can be.

DISCOVERING A SIMPLER WAY

I didn't see it coming. I never expected that a closet clean out would change my life. I loaded up two giant landscaping bags full of my entire wardrobe. I threw them out in front of my house and put up a Facebook message that said:

"Friends, anyone that wants my entire wardrobe—come and get it. It's sitting on my front porch."

Perhaps they thought my sanity was going out the door with those bags, but that was far from the truth. I didn't know it at the time, but when I put out those bags, I also put out the fire that was burning underneath me.

I started to live life more slowly. Some people think it's lazy. But it's not. Living simple is a protective mechanism against the physical disease, mental disorder, and financial debt that are associated with stress and busyness.

I had been living life in the fast lane for too long, and it was time to put on the brakes and pull myself and my family out of the race. This book is the story of how I got started.

I QUIT BUYING

The closet clean out changed everything. First and foremost, it changed the way I view open, white space. White space is physical space, mental space, or time that is open and unoccupied. White space in your living room might look like an empty shelf. White space on your calendar might look like a weekend with nothing planned.

I now welcome white space in my home, on my calendar, and most importantly in my mind. It changed the way I buy. I no longer make purchases on impulse, instead I buy with careful thought and intention.

No more FOMO folks. Not having all-the-things *is a good thing.*

When I put those giant bags on my front porch, a little piece inside of me felt guilty. Because I knew I was onto something new—a fresh start. *A new, lighter life.* Passing those bags full of clearance Target tops and TJ Maxx deals felt like I was passing a torch that I did not want to pass.

Instead, I wanted to share this budding sensation of freedom that I felt being lifted off my shoulders. Which makes me thrilled to be able to share it with you.

I QUIT HUSTLING

My shoulders had been far too heavy for far too long. I spent years carrying a physical and mental load that was too much for me to bear. I spent my days racing from one obligation to the next. I spent my nights tossing and turning making mental to-do lists to start it all over again in the morning.

I spent the early days of motherhood hurrying, hustling, and stressing. Until I realized that living life like you are on fire will in fact leave you burned out.

That brings me to the next thing I didn't see coming: My closet was empty and my calendar was emptier. But oddly enough, this emptiness left me feeling full.

That white space on my calendar wasn't really empty at all. There's nothing in the world I love more than an evening or weekend with nothing planned. Because I now know that "nothing" is far from nothing. "Nothing" means time to intimately connect with my family and myself.

I QUIT HOVERING

I put out the fire on my kids too. I quit parenting out of fear. I quit mothering just to keep them alive. *I wanted to give them more than that.* I let them stray a little bit farther, climb a little bit higher, and yell a little bit louder. I let them learn how to explore their own boundaries.

My kids are learning how to fall, even though it's not always graceful. My job is to kiss those boo-boos and not prevent them. I took my thirteen-month-old out of a crib and into a bed and let him have a taste of unsupervised, yet safe freedom in his bedroom. I decided a five-point harness on a high chair was a little overkill, because I was feeding my kids, not sending them on a rollercoaster ride.

My kids are physically and socially capable and I want to be sure that my attitude and actions communicate that I believe in their abilities. Even though problem-solving between a two- and four-year-old looks a little messy and chaotic, it is their own messy chaos. When I know that they are safe, I choose to let them manage their own conflict.

My life is imperfect, but it is calm, healthy, and happy. My family is living simple and never looking back.

THE SIMPLE MANIFESTO

This book is the culmination of everything I have learned so far—and am still learning—on my journey to a simple family. This two-step program is designed to give parents the tools they need to let go of the clutter in their lives and homes and embrace a more relaxed, fulfilling, and healthy approach to family living.

Starting with the basics, Part One is a guide to getting the home and all your stuff into shape. Just like when I threw out those bags of clothing, physically clearing your space is a huge step on the path to a simpler life. By clearing out your home space, you are not just undertaking a spring cleaning, but embracing a new, lighter way of life.

In Part Two we expand on this simple philosophy and sense of openness and see how this way of living applies to key parenting areas including discipline, play, and scheduling. Instead of parenting through the lens of fear, we can be more intentional about letting our children grow and individuate. When we take a step back, we will find that our children benefit from a "less is more approach" to parenting as well.

We won't get it right all the time, but I can promise you that following the Simple Parenting approach will open you up to a more authentic and fully-lived family life—the family life we all want for our kids and ourselves, the one we just got distracted on the road to. Let's get back on track and discover a simpler way to raise happy, healthy, and successful children.

The Simple Manifesto is—you guessed it—simple:

1. Fear less.
2. Hurry less.
3. Entertain less.
4. Referee less.
5. Buy less.

REAP THE REWARDS

I am not promising a quick-fix or perfect solution—parenting is hard, kids are unpredictable, there will be days when you feel chaotic—but what I can promise is that by adopting this stripped-back approach to family life, you and your children will discover more time, more freedom, more fun. There aren't many things I know for sure. But I do know for sure that slowing down our days will slow down our life. After all, we only get one. We only get one shot at this life and this parenthood stuff. In order to give it our best shot, we need to be able to focus on what matters the most.

With simple living, I have been able to find my way through the weeds and latch on to the relationships and priorities that fill up my cup. And as a result, my cup overflows. With love, happiness, and (on most days) patience.

My life is entirely imperfect and my simple home is sometimes just simply a mess. My kids still freak out and we run out of clean underwear from time to time. But my lens is different. I am striving for a simple and intentional life. The lens I am looking at life through is one of gratitude. From this viewpoint, life is far from perfect, but it's perfectly mine. And for that, I am grateful.

PART ONE
DESIGN
A SIMPLE
FAMILY HOME

GETTING STARTED

First, let's talk about the stuff.

Long before I had a family, I had a clutter problem. Growing up in a working-class home, I was financially responsible from an early age. I worked hard, I bought many of my own clothes, I purchased my first car, and put myself through college and graduate school. I prided myself on being frugal and making good decisions about the way I spent my money.

That also meant I spent too much time stalking the clearance racks and finding the best sales. Even though I was spending less, I was buying just as much. And because I was careful about the way I spent my money, I was also cautious about letting go of the items that I spent my hard-earned money on.

My clutter accrued, and I had a twofold problem: I couldn't put things away and I couldn't throw things away. As a single person, my stuff accumulated fast. But as I started accumulating people (husband, baby #1, baby #2…) I was swimming in it.

And I am not a strong swimmer.

Perhaps we shall say I was doggy paddling in all the stuff.

In my gut, I knew I needed to make better choices. But the day-to-day busyness that occupied my life kept pushing my head under the water.

The clutter in my home only compounded the clutter in my mind. I was drowning in stuff *and* life but I knew I didn't want to take my family down with me.

WHAT DOES SIMPLE FEEL LIKE?

My husband got the first taste of simplicity. My frugal nature had me sign our first-born child up for the cheapest baby class in the neighborhood, which happened to be at the Montessori school across the street. My husband was on duty the first week.

When he came home, he was wide-eyed: "Everything has a place. Each toy has a specific spot that it belongs."

I rolled my eyes.

But then I had my turn. I went the following week and found myself uncomfortable and understimulated. The classroom was serene, perhaps even a bit boring. The caregiver sitting next to me clearly shared the discomfort with the silence and asked for permission to play some music on her phone.

For the first time in my life, I was basking in white space and it was completely foreign to me. I wasn't sure exactly what it meant, but I found myself taking mental notes about my surroundings and the way they made me feel.

The truth? *White space scared me.*

Although I was disarmed by this type of environment, I couldn't help but notice the impact on the children I observed: They were calm and engaged.

And frankly, so was I. I looked forward to this magical little window of time each week where my baby and I could disappear into a tranquil space and be completely present with one another. I knew that I wanted to bottle up all that peace and bring it home—less to clean up, fewer emails that needed responding to, doing barely anything, but creating a bond that meant everything.

I wanted to create a simple home that focused on the people more than the stuff.

Once I tasted simplicity, I knew that I had found the secret sauce that I needed to create a more harmonious life with children. I didn't know what it meant or how to do it. But the next step was to figure out all the ingredients.

WHAT IS A SIMPLE HOME?

The first step in simplifying the family is to simplify the home. A simple home allows us to focus on connection over content. The space we live in serves as a landing pad: When the outside world gets to be too much, we can always return to our home for security. When we feel like hiding out from everyone and everything, we go home.

When we make a life with our children, making a home is a large part of that life. In that life, it's important that we create those safe spaces for our children to grow, develop, and thrive. As a new parent, I knew I wanted this for my children. I wanted to make our home that space for them—a place where they could always come to find comfort and connection.

But sometimes our comfort zone becomes less than comfortable. As parents with full calendars, our homes become even fuller. It becomes even more critical to make our home base a place that allows us to focus and prioritize the things that matter the most.

We want to give our children the world—and that includes all the stuff. But the reality is, they don't need it. *They just need us.* So as you go about making a house a home for your children, be mindful that you need a heckuva lot less stuff than you might think.

Less toys, less clothes, less furniture.

Instead?

More presence, more intention, more patience. **More you.**

CHOOSING FURNITURE AND HOUSEWARES WITH CHILDREN IN MIND

In my quest for creating the simple home, I felt the hard pull towards simplicity. I wanted to get rid of all.the.stuff. But I have a family. I still need stuff.

So I redefined my mission: Pare down to the essentials and create a space that is both beautiful and accessible to the whole family. I wanted to create a home that invited my children to gradually learn how to respect others, themselves, and their environment (both indoor and out). But I also wanted to have nice things.

I aspired to do the following:

- Create a home that was child-friendly, rather than child-proof.
- Give everything a place—that way I could easily clean up and teach my kids how to clean up, too.
- Design a beautiful space in which we all loved to spend time.

I wanted to be intentional about the way that I furnished our family home and give reverence to the impact a home has on the journey of the people living inside of it.

But this doesn't happen overnight. It's a lifelong course that I am still stumbling along. But we can start at home with patience, faith, and trust.

And perhaps a little bit of pixie dust.

THREE STEPS TOWARDS A SIMPLE FAMILY HOME

We all want to make our homes places that are loved, welcoming, and accessible to both children and adults. To do this, the "stuff" needs to be curated and what remains arranged with intention. Our aim is to create a home that is lovely, but functional; safe, but accessible; filled with essentials, but embraces white space.

The three steps below will help you to first rationalize your existing stuff to provide a blank canvas (or at least a clearer canvas) on which to design your simple family home, and secondly to carefully consider the items that you *need*. By adopting an intentional parenting approach that embraces providing children with the freedom and space to grow, we automatically get rid of many of the "things" that are sold to us to keep kids safe or make family life easy (hint: These are marketing ploys, they want us to buy all.the.stuff).

1. Protect your active spaces

At the start of my journey I just had too much stuff. No organizational system could save me. *I was in too deep. Whenever I needed something I first had to dig through a thousand other things I didn't need to find it.* A clean out and careful curation of our home was the first step. I kept all the things that my family used and loved, then re-homed the rest.

The first step in simplifying your home is to recognize and protect your active spaces. Our homes are actively used spaces: People live in them and it should show. As an actively used space, your home should only contain actively used items. When you start mixing in unused and unloved items into these spaces, that's when things get messy.

When you open my kitchen cabinet, you will find only the items I actively use. That means I don't have to sort through twelve types of beans when I really only ever use the black ones. When you open my closet door you will find only the clothes I actively wear. My favorite pair of jeans isn't buried within twenty-four pairs that I never wear. When you walk into the playroom, you

will see only the toys with which my children actively engage. That means carefully chosen items can be easily accessed to create and innovate by children of different genders and different ages.

When sorting through your belongings, examine each item and ask yourself a question: Is this an active item, a storage item, or a share-the-love item? This question then provides a guide to what should be done with that item:

Active items belong in active spaces

Items that we use daily or weekly belong in the active spaces of our home. These are the zones of the house that we use regularly, for example the mud-room where we drop our shoes and coats, the kitchen pantry, and clothing closets. *These spaces need to only contain actively used items.*

Storage items belong in storage spaces

On the other hand, items that we use infrequently belong in storage spaces. These are areas that we place things we do not use on a regular basis. That might mean the pan we roast our turkey in twice a year or the Easter baskets. A select number of mementos and pieces you love may belong in this area as well. This might be in the attic, a storage closet, or perhaps under the bed. The items are still easily accessible for when you need them, but not cluttering up the active areas of your home.

Share-the-love items

If we don't actively use the items, nor do we ever pull them out of storage, then they belong in a 'share-the-love' box. These are items that will leave your home and find love and worth in the possession of another family. Items that belong in this box are children's books and clothing that are outgrown, the four extra crib sheets you ordered "just in case", and the shoes you "outgrew" in your last pregnancy.

As I moved through this process my home was transformed. The share-the-love boxes went to families in need, the storage items were carefully posited for future uses, and the curated remaining active items started to live their best lives in our home.

Once I got rid of the stuff, I stopped digging and started living.

2. Create a child-friendly home

Once you have curated your stuff, you are ready to turn your home into a space that is safe and welcoming for your children, allowing them to be active participants in all aspects of family life. To do that, it is important to start giving them small amounts of independence starting in the earliest of months.

For our family, that meant the first child was standing up washing vegetables at the kitchen counter as soon as he could walk. Our second child was sleeping soundly in her big-kid bed before she was weaned. Our toys are all down low so that the children can both access them easily and put them away (and they usually do!).

I absolutely don't say this to brag, I say this to illustrate the fact that children are capable human beings that can do far more than we expect when they are given the time and white space they need to grow. This will look different for every family depending on what they are comfortable with and how they live and play.

The key is that we want our kids to be able to move about freely in the home without fear of injury and to create a home that is child-friendly rather than child-proof. But in today's world, child-proofing is big business. There are gadgets galore to keep children out of unwanted territories. While I am a firm believer in making a home safe from life-threatening risks, putting a child-proof lock on the toilet seat to keep your kid from splashing around is more convenience than critical.

For me, I wanted to move away from child-proofing and convenience parenting. My mindset was that if I don't want my kids to get into my make-up drawer, I need to teach them to stay out of it. So we covered the electrical outlets and secured the furniture to the walls. Then we capitalized on all the teachable moments we had as our kids learned about boundaries and limits in the home.

If that sounds like a lot of work, that's because it was. Intentional parenting, my friends, is work. What it does do however, is release you from the truckload of items that the stores tell us are essential for a safe family home. With this philosophy in mind, you can reassess your current home environment to see if there are any unnecessary items you can remove, and also take forward when considering new purchases or updates.

3. Don't fear the breakables

An extension of step two, when considering how to furnish our homes or choosing homewares we need to let go of the fear of breakables; the automatic reach for the wipe-clean, indestructible option. I am here to tell you two things: First, you can have nice things, and second, your house doesn't have to look like a plastic three-ring-kid-circus.

When I registered for my first baby, I went a little wild. My list had all.the. things. But even then, I questioned the need to kid-ify my home. I wanted it to look like a place that adults loved, but welcomed children as well. I wanted us to coexist in an environment that didn't resemble plastic hell.

More seasoned mothers warned me: "Until further notice, you cannot have nice things. You must hide the breakables. You must remove the valuables," and I started to wonder if I was having a baby or preparing for an armed robbery! But I am here to tell you that you can coexist: You can have nice things and children can survive with relatively few things. And not just survive, but thrive.

A baby does not need a high chair covered in wild-colored, tropical-print plastics (unless of course, **you** love it). A baby does not need toys that simultaneously make noise, vibrate, and light up. A baby does not, in fact, need all.the.things.

When we simplify the environment of our children we improve their ability to focus, decrease stress, and give them more opportunities for creativity and innovation. We also give them opportunities to practice independence and caring for the items they love.

If you give a child forty toys, they will litter the floor and get stepped upon. If you give a child four toys, they will be treasured, valued, and cared for.

I knew that I wanted to make my home a place that was loved and accessible to both children and adults. When given the opportunity to learn, children are capable of caring for fragile and delicate things from a very young age.

Children actually benefit from toys and items that are simple in color and design. We know that children focus better in less distracting environments, so keeping their spaces at home simple is an important piece of that process.

By curating the number of objects that exist in our home, it makes it a lot easier to clean up. That means fewer toys, clothes, and random items scattered across the floor. It also means fewer piles in the bottom of the closet. When everything has its place, it becomes easy to take good care of the items that remain.

So yes, you can have nice things.

Just not white sofas, never buy the white sofas.

How to tackle a clear out

I can tell you firsthand that a *clutter-free* home is the first step toward a *chaos-free* home. Reducing the amount of clutter in your home will allow you to spend less time tidying and more time focusing on what matters the most: *the people*.

Clearing out the home is the first step to living a simpler life.

I spent years trying to organize and move my stuff around until I finally figured out the root of the problem: *too much stuff*. Therefore, I am confident that tackling a home clean out will put you on the path to simplifying your family life.

Here are the five steps to executing a clean out:

1. **Take out all the stuff.** Start with a single space and empty it. The space should look like the day you moved in (leave the furniture!). Seeing the space as brand new will shine a light at the end of the tunnel.

2. **Select only the most vital objects one at a time.** Only the active items used and loved should be kept accessible in the home. Items used less frequently should be placed into storage or put into a Share-the-love box (see page 43). Carefully replenish the space until it reaches a point where it feels light, yet comfortable. It should feel calm and relaxing in this room.

3. **Box up the rest of the stuff and put it into "purgatory."** You don't have to discard everything just yet, but do put it out of the room. Choose a space that is out of the way, yet visible. *You don't want to hide it away and forget it exists.*

4. **Live in the simplified space.** Spend some time living decluttered. Get a sense of how it feels to live lighter. But be warned, it's addicting in the best kind of way.

5. **One month later.** Pay a *brief* visit to the purgatory. Are there any items you absolutely need or want to save? If not, drive them straight away for donations. (Hint: Avoid indefinite purgatory in the trunk of your car.)

Meet Erica Layne

Getting kids on board with big life changes doesn't always come easy. That's why I invited my friend Erica Layne to share more about this topic. She and her family reside in the San Francisco Bay area. Erica has three kids and has been on a journey toward minimalism and simplicity for many years. She's a writer, researcher, and a lover of self-help resources. Erica is the voice behind The Life on Purpose Movement and the author of the book *The Minimalist Way: Minimalism Strategies to Declutter Your Life and Make Room for Joy*. Her work inspires individuals all over the world to live simply and have self-compassion.

So, I asked Erica...

How can we get kids onboard with simple living?

Here's how she answered:

It was 5th period, after lunch on a hot Arizona day, so the air conditioner was pumping full force. My English teacher had written the words "show, don't tell" in big, block letters on the whiteboard.

As a full-on English nerd even at age fifteen, I was immediately struck by the concept. My mind ran through several of my favorite books, connecting that what made each of these stories so special was the author's ability to "show."

I've grown up a *bit* since my sophomore English class. I went away to college, got married, moved half a dozen times, wrote a book about minimalism, and had three kids—the oldest of whom is now eleven.

In my decade of parenting, I've learned that "show, don't tell" applies to so much more than writing a short story for your English teacher. In fact, it's become one of my most relied-on parenting practices—especially when it comes to teaching my kids about living simple. I don't want to *tell* my kids how to live; I want to *show* them how *I* choose to live—and how much joy I find in it.

Like any parent, I have hopes for my kids, *of course*. But I recognize that they are each going to take their own paths. It's part of the design. I also know that my kids tend to build up resistance when I'm too prescriptive about something. (I swear that the more I tell them to put the toilet seat down, the more they leave it *up*...)

So, I'm taking a backdoor approach to getting my kids onboard with my minimalist way of life. Here are a handful of practices that allow me to *show* my passion for minimalism and invite them to join me in the simple life, without directly *telling* them how to live.

1. Incorporate principles of simple living into your family values

Years ago, our family spent a month honing in on our family values—and our values include living simply. We talk about this concept often and try to live it as a family, but I think the key is that they are a part of a larger whole—they are a part of our combined family identity.

2. Be deliberate about the messages you display in your home

I believe that the words and images we have on our walls seep into the hearts of our children. There's power in hanging photos of a favorite family vacation or nature outing—or well-loved words that support your minimalist values.

3. Watch for subtle teaching moments

When your child spends her hard-earned money on a toy that ends up forgotten in a corner within only a few weeks, casually point out how quickly the excitement of a new item wears off. When your kids go to environments that are different to your home, ask them how they felt while there. Take advantage of small teaching moments in the middle of regular life but do it gently and without judgment of their answers.

4. Talk up the joy you experience from living with less

If there's one thing my kids know about me, it's that I love a half-empty closet. They know that I enjoy getting dressed, because I like my (limited) options. They know that a calendar with plenty of white space makes me lightheaded with happiness. They know that I go at my own pace—and that the alignment I feel inside makes life that much richer for me.

Don't hesitate to share your joy over the way you live. Maybe, just maybe, your kids will want that same joy for themselves.

CREATING A CAPSULE WARDROBE FOR KIDS

My kids have capsule wardrobes. At first, you might think that sounds fancy. But rest assured, there is nothing fancy about it. Instead, creating a capsule wardrobe can be a simple and smart decision for the whole family.

A few years ago I got rid of my whole wardrobe and started afresh. It was simultaneously scary, exciting, and liberating. My closet was transformed from this giant, messy storage space to an active space that held a few select pieces of clothing that I loved to wear. Each day I approach the space with a smile and select clothing without a touch of decision fatigue.

Having a smaller, well-curated wardrobe is a decision that many successful individuals have made—including former US President Barack Obama who famously alternated between two different suits each day of his presidency.

I decided that if the leader of the free world could survive with fewer choices, so could my children. I knew the next step in simplifying was taking on their wardrobes, and sure enough the change in my children's wardrobe made my brain and my house feel lighter.

I used to amass my kids' clothes in a haphazard fashion. Casual drive-bys of the kids' section at Target where I spotted something cute and tossed it into the cart. Impulse buys at the random boutique I stumbled upon. Hand-me-downs by the giant bag from well-meaning friends and family. One thing was for sure, my kids would never go naked (at least, not by my doing anyways—however, nudity is embraced by my two-year-old).

Now, when buying for my children's capsule wardrobes, I make purchases with intention. I strive to compile a simple and smart collection of clothing that is sustainable, flexible, and affordable.

Here is how to create a capsule wardrobe for your kids:

KEEP IT SIMPLE

Fewer clothes makes life simpler—in all aspects including both shopping and daily dressing. When we put together a child's wardrobe, *it is* possible to keep it simple. It can be tempting to slowly accumulate clothing on our own whim or the whim of our children—but by being intentional we can ensure that we are selecting fewer pieces that are higher quality and flexible to fit with many different looks.

Keep the shopping simple by minimizing the number of stores you visit. Select one or two stores that fit the style of your children and family. If you select items from one or two stores, you will ensure that not only is the style streamlined, but also the sizing. Clothing from various stores face a wild variation of sizes.

A well-curated wardrobe will help to eliminate battles in getting dressed each day. When you have fewer pieces that all fit well, you will ensure that children can easily choose comfortable and appropriate clothing for whatever event lies ahead.

MAKE IT SUSTAINABLE

Children go through clothing more rapidly than adults. They grow, they get dirty, they change taste…in all, they require more shopping. This makes it more important to think about sustainability when putting together a capsule wardrobe for them.

When you shop sustainably for children, it means that you focus on buying pieces that have either been worn before or will have the longevity to be passed along after your family is finished with it. Children cycle through clothing more quickly, therefore to prevent excessive clothing waste it is important to assess the lifespan of clothing:

- Was it worn by another child before it reached yours?
- Will it last and hold the value to be passed on to another family after yours has finished?

When we simplify our homes, we start to become careful shoppers and conscious consumers. That means we think about the impact of our purchases beyond the time they spend in our homes.

PRIORITIZE COMFORT

Children are drawn to comfort. They prefer soft, easy-to-wear fabrics that are easy to put on and take off. So focus your search on natural, loose-fitting materials with a simple design.

My daughter is a natural minimalist when it comes to clothing. Once she finds a comfortable piece that jives with her current interests she will insist on wearing the item every single day.

When you've got a good, cozy thing going, why change it?

When creating a capsule wardrobe for your child, keep in mind their clothing preferences and how they use the clothes they wear. There is no point buying that adorable cardigan you love if your tot is going to find the buttons tricky and the fabric uncomfortable.

ADOPT A FLEXIBLE COLOR SCHEME

When selecting clothing stick with a flexible color scheme. My four-year-old uses his shirt as a perma-napkin so I prefer to stick with dark colors that don't stain as easily. Choose neutral-colored bottoms that can be mixed and matched with any tops.

BUT WHAT ABOUT THE LAUNDRY?

I know your next question: What about laundry? I do laundry every day. *Don't groan.* Let me tell you, it isn't as bad as it might sound. Through the course of the day my family of four generally creates a small load worth of laundry. Each night after we change into pajamas all the dirty clothes go into the washing machine. I switch it into the dryer before bedtime and then I fold it the following evening when I am starting the next load of clothing.

That's it. *No piles of clothes building up for a week.* Rarely do we run out of clean socks. *But most importantly, I have more white space.* I'm not spending an entire Sunday afternoon catching up with laundry. I also don't have dirty clothes strewn across my house...ever. Because if it's dirty, it's in the washing machine. If it's clean, it's in the drawers. Trust me on this one and try it out. *Everyday laundry is kind of awesome.* It's also just smart.

CHOOSE CLOTHES YOU LOVE

Be sure to choose clothes that both you and your children love: Speaking from experience, if you don't want her to wear the pink tutu dress every day, don't buy the pink tutu dress. Be fully prepared that you may have a natural minimalist who loves to put her favorites on repeat.

IT CAN BE AFFORDABLE AND SMART

Buying fewer clothes can be affordable, but not always. I spend more money on quality over quantity. That means I buy fewer pieces, but those pieces are often higher-quality, higher-cost items.

Choosing to purchase fewer pieces not only reduces the waste that we are contributing to landfills, but it also reduces the stress that accompanies clothing overwhelm in family homes. Certain clothing brands hold good resale value as well, so I stick with those brands when possible. That way I can consign a few pieces to purchase the next season's capsule.

Having fewer choices when it comes to clothing will dramatically reduce the amount of "stuff" in your home. You will have fewer drawers to sort through, spend less time digging for what you are looking for, and overall your kids will be both happier and cuter as a result. I know mine are.

Plus parents too—how to declutter your own wardrobe

I got rid of my wardrobe and never looked back. Not only did my closet change, but so did the way I feel about getting dressed and venturing out into the world each day. Today, my wardrobe is tiny. But I look and feel more put together than ever before. If you are interested in taking the plunge yourself, here are five steps to get you started:

1. **Pick a number for which to aim.** When you start decluttering your clothes, it helps it to set a number to aim for. I went for forty-five: twenty tops and/or dresses, ten bottoms, and fifteen pairs of shoes.

2. **Choose your color palette.** Pick four to six basic colors to build your closet around. By keeping the colors consistent your wardrobe will be more flexible. It will be easy to mix-and-match any of the pieces.

3. **Research some looks**. I am fashion-challenged. Therefore, I started paying attention to the advertisements. I subscribed to email updates from my favorite stores and looked at the way the models put pieces together and accessorized. I took notes on the way they tucked in their shirts and the way they rolled their pants. This gives you both the confidence to know what you like, and the know-how to put your capsule wardrobe together in all sorts of great combinations.

4. **Empty your closet.** Take a deep breath. Now empty your whole closet. You will start with an empty space and then add only a select few pieces back in one at a time.

5. **Go shopping with a plan.** Figure out exactly what you are looking for before you head out to fill in the remaining closet gaps. Do your research: Make a list of the pieces you want to purchase ahead of time and where they are available.

Making this change means no more impulse purchases. No more grab-and-go when you pass through a department store. No more perusing the clearance racks for something that is "just too cheap *or* too cute to pass up."

This is your first step toward buying clothing with intention.

HOW TO MINIMIZE THE TOYS

When it comes to toys, there is a dichotomy in our society. The vast majority of seasoned parents will tell you that children just need a few cardboard boxes and some bubble wrap to be happy. But those same parents are still buying toys for their children.

A lot of toys.

Even though we see children gravitating toward the refrigerator box more than the plastic light-up spaceship, we still buy the spaceships. We keep buying toys because there is an underlying conviction in today's society that children need toys to be happy. Therefore, one might presume this means that children who have *more* toys also experience *more* happiness.

But that's actually not true. Children who have fewer toys are less stressed and more creative.

Do you know the feeling you get when you walk into a clean and tidy room? It feels calm. It feels like a place that you want to spend a lot of time.

Our children feel that too, but more intensely. Young children are sensitive to overstimulation and benefit from simplified spaces even more than adults. That means children who have less toy clutter are more focused, more innovative, and calmer overall.

I know this because I have helped thousands of families declutter toys and the response is universal: **Kids play better and behave better when they have fewer toys.**

But there are other benefits as well.

When you have fewer toys children learn to play more independently. The toys are easier to see and access—therefore children can initiate and lengthen periods of independent play without the need to call for parental support. Research shows that having fewer toys also evokes more creativity in children—which means that children will be satisfied to create and play more frequently and for a longer duration of time.

When parents move toward minimizing toys, they often feel a classic battle between the head and the heart. In your head, mass media and marketing is telling you that your kids need all the toys. But if you are reading this book, your heart is probably telling you that your children are actually better off with fewer toys.

Follow your heart.

THE INTENTIONAL APPROACH

When approaching your kids' toys, it is important that you do so with a positive attitude. Downsizing the toys is good for children. But it can be scary, and it can be met with resistance.

You don't have to commit to re-homing the toys immediately. I encourage you to send the toys on a vacation for a few weeks—pack them up and move them from the active space in your home to a storage space temporarily. Experience living with less and watch how your children play and take care of their well-curated belongings.

Just try it.

When you start to scale back on toys you should approach the process with a positive tone of voice. The way that you approach this change will make a world of difference in how children respond.

Avoid the following statements:

- "You never take care of this stuff so we are getting rid of it."
- "You don't play with your toys anyways, so we are going to give them to kids who actually appreciate them."

Instead, try this:

- "We are going to give your play space a makeover so you can easily see the toys and play with them in new ways."
- "We are going to send some of the toys on vacation for a while so we can see what it feels like to focus on your favorite things."

Remember, as the parent you are steering the ship, but you have to get your kids onboard before you can set sail.

OBSERVE YOUR CHILDREN

When you are preparing to minimize toys, it's important to be an observer. When you observe your children's play, you can better understand which toys bring value to your home. These are the toys that your children gravitate toward most often and play with constructively.

We want to keep the toys that bring value to our home. Young children need toys that provide opportunities for language, movement, and creativity. That's why I prefer to choose toys that meet the 90/10 rule.

Toys that bring value to our children will simply support the play, rather than doing all the work. So when you observe your children play, pay attention to toys that they are engaged with and which create "work" (i.e. learning opportunities).

The 90/10 rule for toys is that the child should be doing 90 percent of the work and the toy should be doing 10 percent of the work. Here's an example:

- A push-button musical toy requires the child to simply push a button to play music. The toy is doing 90 percent of the work, and the child is only doing 10 percent.

- A tambourine requires the child to move, shake, and create rhythm and tempo. The child is doing 90 percent of the work, and the toy is only doing 10 percent.

SELECT THE TOYS

We know that our children learn through play. Therefore, it is important to understand that their play spaces become de facto learning zones. The toys that we choose should be a joint effort with our children—toys that our children love and that will evoke opportunities for growth and development.

Here are four questions to keep in mind when selecting which toys to keep:

1. Does my kid LOVE and engage with this toy?
2. Does this toy offer opportunity for my kids to innovate and create?
3. Will this toy encourage movement, either small, refined movements with the hands or large whole-body movements?
4. Is this toy versatile? Can it be used in many different ways by children of different ages and genders?

When you use these questions, you will be thinking more intentionally about the toys that you are bringing into your home. You will be ensuring that these items add value to your life as a family. Thoughtful, intentional buying in childhood will set the example for our children as they grow.

ARRANGE THE TOYS

The way that we arrange our children's toys has a direct impact on the way that children engage with the toys. When you have relatively few toys, they can be easily arranged so that they are accessible and visible. I prefer to keep a small amount of curated toys out on shelves in trays or shallow bins.

When toys are visible, it will ensure that children can see all of the available options and quickly make a choice to engage in play. It will also ensure that clean up is straightforward, *because everything has a place.*

On the contrary, when you have a lot of toys you tend to pile them into large toy boxes and bins. While this makes clean up simple, it also buries toys. When toys are buried it prevents children from being able to see them and they will engage with the toys less frequently.

Alternatively, if the overfull toy box or bin is a manageable size and can be dumped by small people, children will in fact dump toys to be able to see what's at the bottom. The result: Toys all over the floor getting stepped upon. When the toys cover the floor, chaos ensues.

That feeling of calm that comes in a tidy room quickly dissipates when toy clutter takes over. Even children don't want to be in chaotic spaces like this—so you will often see the children flee the room quickly as the floor becomes covered, then you may find them hanging on your leg while you are cooking dinner.

START THE DETOX

When we make the transition to fewer toys, we will see major changes in the way our children play. Our children will enjoy spending time in their play spaces and will venture to them more frequently. They will also start to value the toys that they have—because it's easier to take care of ten toys as opposed to 100 toys. But there may be a detox period. Children who have been inundated with too many toys may need a period of time to get back to the basics of play.

There's a good chance they won't walk into a simplified play space and start running with new ideas for pretend play. Instead they might ask for more screen time. This is because play is the work of childhood, and it takes just that: work. High-quality play involves many opportunities for language, movement, socialization, and creativity.

A kid that isn't accustomed to these things can find it overwhelming and exhausting at first. If you find your children are a bit confused or even bored—let them experience those feelings. Play is hard work, but the skills necessary to play are innate within children. Some just need extra time and white space to practice and learn how to enjoy it.

Let them be bored; their innovation will astound you.

MAINTAIN IT

Anyone can declutter, but staying decluttered is the hard part. After you have removed the majority of the toys your children will begin to adjust. They will detox. Then they will get back to the basics of play.

This is the best part—watching them grow, engage, and learn through play.

After that, you can make the decision about what to do with the rest of the toys. I will warn you, when families leave all the excess toys in a storage space they slowly drift back into the active space. I strongly recommend you don't leave them in a storage space and instead donate them to a charity shop for another family to enjoy.

After you have experienced the change in your children's play, it will take intentional buying to stick with it. To stay decluttered, protect your active spaces. Be sure that you are only bringing in items that add value and maintain the feeling of lightness and calm that children thrive within.

How to choose toys

When choosing toys, we try to find toys that are durable and versatile. Choosing great toys will cut down on waste and clutter. But it will also increase the opportunities for creativity, movement, and learning for children.

To strike a balance, I recommend keeping 75 percent open toys and 25 percent closed toys. Open toys are toys that can be used by a variety of children who are different ages and genders. Closed toys are more limited in the ages and interests for which they are designed.

An example of an open toy is a set of wooden blocks. They can be stacked, sorted, counted, or turned into pretend food. The options are endless. They are an open, durable toy that can be used by children of any age.

Closed toys can be great as well—an example is a six-piece jigsaw puzzle. *But...there is only one way to put it together.* Once it is mastered, it will no longer be of interest to your child.

If your home contains more open toys, your children will have less clutter and more opportunities for play. The toys will also hold their interest for longer periods of time. Here are three of my favorite open toys.

Magnatiles. These toys have been turned into a balance beam, carwash, and train tracks. They have a magnetic quality about them—as in you won't be able to put them down. They are a favorite of kids aged two to 100.

Wooden house. A plain wooden house can set the stage for endless options of pretend play. When you have a simple structure like this, children can pretend it is a barn, a firehouse, a doll house, etc.

Silk scarves. Simple silk scarves make excellent capes, dresses, and bandanas. Having a few of these scarves on hand will provide endless opportunities for creativity and imagination.

When you buy open, durable toys you will find that their lifespan has unlimited potential. Intentionally buying toys is just smart.

How to organize books

I love books. Especially children's books. The time spent reading books with my kids is special. The books we read over and over become very special— sometimes even a little sentimental and hard to let go of.

We know that children benefit greatly from reading aloud with their parents, so having books in the home is important. But it can be easy to slip into book chaos. That means books all over the floor, getting stepped on and ripped up.

Not only do I want to avoid book chaos, but I also believe that we have a social responsibility to re-home books that we are no longer reading. There are many children in the world who lack access to books at home. Our surplus may be another family's treasure.

Here are the four steps to organizing kids' books:

1. **Choose the Book Headquarters.** We have a main command center located in a closet. This is where the vast majority of the books reside. From this library we choose a selection of titles to be readily available to the kids at any one time. Young children have a difficult time managing *too many* books, so we help them out by keeping the quantity available to a minimum. For our headquarters, I chose a closet that is near to our living space, out of reach but not quite out of sight.

2. **Minimize your books.** Children need to own fewer books than we realize, so start a share-the-love box and fill it up. There is value in borrowing books from the library to learn how to care for and return things that belong to others. There is also developmental value in re-reading the same books to better understand vocabulary and storylines. Don't be afraid to re-home books, they will be better loved in the hands of another family than packed away in a storage space. Let's borrow more and buy less.

3. **Designate access points.** I want my children to value books and
literature. By having fewer books we will encourage our children to put
them away and take better care of them with ease. To do this, I have
created access points for books at key points in our home. That means
we have a select number of books on small shelves in the children's
bedrooms and in the playroom. The rest live in the Book Headquarters.

4. **Rotate the books.** We regularly rotate the books in the access points.
That means we keep the literature selection fresh while at the same
time keeping the options minimal. At any time our children are free
to request new books from headquarters—and we frequently move
them around.

Believe me when I say that more is less, *even when it comes to books
at home.*

How to manage gifts

When we approached the pavilion near the playground, the birthday boy approached us. We came bearing a card with a gift certificate inside for a magazine subscription. He glanced quickly at the envelope and then at us. "Where's my gift?" he asked.

Now I don't blame the kid, gifts are super fun. In fact, they can be blindingly fun. They are fun for the givers and the receivers. But too many gifts can become distracting from the real gifts that surround special events: Like the togetherness and company of people we love.

All families have values. In our family, we value living with less. This means that my kids don't get many wrapped, tangible gifts for birthdays and holidays. On birthday invitations I write, "No gifts please, your presence is the present."

Sure, maybe it's a little corny. But it's true.

I want my children to value presence over presents.

This is an ongoing conversation with family members who are regular gifts-givers. Although we don't forbid gifts, we try to lead by example and set the tone for special gatherings by emphasizing other types of abundance: family, life, love, religion, and togetherness.

I want my children to uphold our family values. To teach them to do that, I have to stand up for those values myself. That *might* mean having slightly awkward conversations with well-intentioned gift-givers.

Approach with honesty, kindness, and love. Here is an example of words you could use:

"Our kids love spending time with you and I have enjoyed seeing your relationship grow. I fear that too many packages may distract them from appreciating all the wonderful gifts you bring as a person. I want them to look forward to special time with you *more* than they do gifts. How can we work together to keep them focused on the important stuff?"

This conversation might need to happen more than once—try to be patient, especially if this family value runs counter to the values of the gift-giver. *Express gratitude and count your blessings for the people who love you.*

HOW TO SIMPLIFY MEAL TIMES

When it comes to feeding our children, it can be very easy to overparent. We have the best of intentions. We know exactly what we should be feeding our children: vegetables (*lots* of leafy greens), lean proteins, wild fish, whole grains, etc. *I get it.*

There is no shortage of information in the world about *what* to feed our children. The problem lies in *how* to feed our children. Even if you are blessed to have access to all the healthiest foods, if your children refuse to eat them then you have a conundrum.

As a reformed picky eater, I know this personally. I didn't start eating vegetables until I was nineteen years old. I knew I wanted things to be different with my own kids, so I approached the feeding process with intention. It was also an added bonus that my doctoral research in Child Wellness placed an emphasis on feeding young children, meaning I came into the feeding process fully prepared.

And I want to tell you, feeding children doesn't have to be complicated.

Even though this is true, many of the best parents I know struggle with meal times. As intentional parents, we want to be sure to give our children choices so they feel empowered in life. But then we start giving them choices for meal times and it spirals out of control. Suddenly it's a pattern of PB&J alternated with mac and cheese and a side of strawberry yogurt.

The question remains: How do we empower our children to eat well, while simultaneously putting limits and boundaries on meal times?

The answer? We need to define our role in the feeding process and put simple plans into place.

As parents, we want meal times to be pleasant. Our days revolve around meals and we value the time spent at the table with our family. When meal times are pleasant, not only does it make life easier and more joyful, but according to research it actually helps our children to eat better foods. When meal times are unpleasant, we feel like we are failing at one of our fundamental responsibilities: feeding our family.

First, we have to believe in our children. Next, we have to implement simple and consistent boundaries around meal times. And lastly, we have to stick to our job description.

1. YOU GOTTA BELIEVE

Here's your new mantra. Say it aloud, say it in your head.

"My children will eat well."

You must believe at your core that your children will learn to eat well and meal times can be joyful. There's no secret juju to this (ok, well maybe there is a little juju). Here's why this works:

It transforms our actions

When we believe our children are capable of eating well we will continue to serve them non-preferred foods. Research shows that children need numerous exposures to foods before they begin to accept them. Yet our

tendency as parents is to stop buying and serving foods that our children refuse. Keep serving up the good stuff—over and over again.

It lifts the pressure

When we believe our children will eat, we feel less pressure to "make it happen." The result is that we will exude less pressure when we are feeding our children. Research shows us that pressuring children to eat will not result in eating better, but it may result in a difficult relationship with food.

It halts our sneakiness

The feeding relationship between a parent and child is based on trust. This relationship is more valuable than the nutrients that come from hiding vegetables among other foods. Vitamin deficiencies in childhood are less common than we think due to the large amount of fortification that occurs in many of the foods they eat. If we want to teach children to eat well then we need to be transparent in the food we are serving and our expectations.

2. IMPLEMENT SIMPLE BOUNDARIES AND STRUCTURE

It's important to establish expectations for meal times. Not only is it important, but it is possible.

Limit the snacks

In our house, children are permitted to eat as much as they want at meal times. However, the size of snacks is restricted. This is important because when children eat snacks too frequently or in large quantities it has a direct impact on their appetite for the following meal time.

Many children today rarely experience hunger due to the frequent snacking. Children who come to the table a bit hungry will eat better. That means they will eat a larger quantity of foods and more of a variety of foods. Now that might be a controversial statement, and in no way am I suggesting that we let our children starve. But hunger is an important biological cue that our body gives us to know when to eat.

Let's welcome hunger and teach our children that it's not something to fear. It's normal and it's healthy. *Hunger tells our body when to eat and helps us to establish healthy eating patterns.*

Use meal windows

In our house, we swear by meal windows. Dinner time is no longer the exact time that we sit down at the table. It's a two-hour window of time. A meal window is an hour before the meal is served and an hour after the meal is served.

Having a meal window will change the way you react to your kids requesting other foods before or after the time a meal is served. The next time you are cooking dinner and your kid is begging for a snack twenty minutes before it's ready, remember: It's dinnertime. The next time you have just cleaned up the meal and they are asking for yogurt, remember: It's dinnertime.

In the hour before the meal is served, children are allowed to snack on foods used in the prep. If we are having roasted carrots, then they can snack on the raw carrots. Other than that, they need to wait until the meal is served.

Likewise, food consumption during the hour after the meal is served is limited to the select foods served at dinner. That means they can indulge on the leftovers or the food that remains on their plate—but you're not serving up something *more* delicious immediately after dinner.

Don't force them to stay at the table

There's no way around it, children will be irritable if you force them to stay at the table. This runs counter to the idea that the time at the table should be pleasant and joyful. Don't get me wrong, it is possible to keep them at the table if you use an electronic device, toys, or threats. But think twice: **Are those truly the dynamics that you want to set up for family time?** If not, then let them go. When they are through eating they can be excused from the table. A large part of having the family spend time together at the table is enjoying and participating in the conversation. Until children come of age where they can be active participants in family conversation and debates,they will easily tire of sitting at the table.

Trust in the process. As children grow and become more conversational, they will want to be a part of meal times for longer periods. This will be a gradual process that will increase as they *enjoy* spending this time with the people they love. Let them come into this on their own time.

3. HONOR YOUR JOB DESCRIPTION

As parents we have an important role in the feeding process. We have a specific job description. Our children also have a specific job description. We need to respect one another's roles.

Job description

Parents choose the food that is to be served, and children choose how much to eat and whether or not they will eat it.

This job description is derived from Ellyn Satter's principle called the Division of Responsibilities (www.ellynsatterinstitute.org). Ellyn has been researching this phenomenon for years. Her research points to the fact that we as parents need to respect our own responsibilities and avoid stepping on the toes of our kids.

That means we simply serve up the good stuff—we are not short-order cooks. Then once we have done our job, we need to let our children do theirs. Their job is to make a choice about how much of the good stuff they are going to eat (or allowing them to opt out altogether).

Watch your language

Sometimes we accidentally classify foods for our kids. When a child chooses not to eat a food, we are quick to declare it a "disliked food." When a child readily eats a food, we are quick to declare it a "liked food."

This seems trivial, but it's important: Children's food preferences are dynamic. *They change like the wind.* We have to be careful about how we talk about them. When we frequently discuss foods that our kids don't like, they are less likely to turn a corner and come around to it. Remember, just because a child chooses not to eat a food today, doesn't mean they won't eat it tomorrow.

At our core we have to believe in them and let our language reflect that.

Babies can eat real food, too

Starting young with simple meal-time routines can set up your family for success. While it can be easy to reach for the prepackaged baby foods—it can also be easy (and important) to feed babies real food. The research shows us that in the first year of life children are the most open to trying new foods. After the first birthday, the tendencies toward picky eating can start to set in. Here are three tips to get you off to the best start possible:

1. Before one, just for fun

Before the first birthday, the primary source of nutrition for a baby should come from breastmilk or formula. That means that for the first twelve months, solid foods are to be slowly introduced as part of a learning process. Because we are not relying on these foods to nourish our babies, we don't have to worry about how much they eat. That makes this window of time ideal for starting good habits. Babies learn quickly that they will get an alternative food if they refuse the first offering. When she turns her head at the green beans, don't pull out the pears. *This is the gateway to short-order cooking.* When she refuses a food, don't stress—she is filling up on milk to get the food stuff anyways. Remember to stick to your job description, even in the earliest of months.

2. Consider the tastes

Breastmilk is sweet and as a result, babies are naturally inclined to like sweet flavors. Most babies will slowly develop preferences toward salty and sour foods as well, but bitter is the last and most difficult taste preference to develop. It just so happens that many vegetables fall into this category: broccoli, spinach, asparagus, etc. Remember how the first year is when babies are most likely to accept new foods? Let's be sure to serve up lots of bitter foods during this time to develop the preference for this flavor. The longer we wait, the more challenging it may become.

3. Provide the textures

We used to think that toothless babies needed liquid purees. But now we know that those toothless gums can be powerful. I am a strong believer in Baby-Led Weaning. BLW is an approach coined by Gill Rapley (www.rapleyweaning.com). Gill advocates for feeding babies whole foods from the very beginning.

This is an ideal way to expose children to new textures. It should come without surprise that getting children to eat a variety of textures may become more difficult after the first birthday, too. So if you have a baby, get started!

Simplify meal planning

When it comes to preparing meals for my family, I can get overwhelmed quickly. I decluttered and got rid of my cookbooks due to my preference for online recipes. Yet I suffer decision fatigue when I even think about Pinterest. *I feel like I have tried it all when it comes to meal planning.* Every family has unique needs, but here are the three methods that I use at home to simplify meal planning:

1. Reverse meal planning

This is the easiest method of all—because it doesn't require a recipe. Here's how it works: Go to the grocery store and buy a variety of proteins and vegetables. Aim to buy what's on sale—because that usually corresponds with what is in season. Then choose a cooking method, for us it's usually either roasting or steaming. Top with olive oil, salt, and pepper and cook until done. Even though the methods are the same, each day feels unique because it brings different foods.

2. One-pot meals

I swear by one-pot meal recipes. These are recipes where you throw everything into one pot (or pan) and cook it altogether. This does require a bit of recipe finding (search: one-pot meals), but the labor of cooking is reduced significantly. And my favorite part of all? *There is truly only one pot to wash.*

3. Meal planning service

I never imagined a meal planning service would work for me, but much to my surprise I love it. I use a service that sends me a list of recipes each week. I receive a grocery list all written out for me and a detailed plan of how to prep the foods. It allows me to prep a whole week of meals in advance so that the meals are nearly ready when it comes time to serve my family.

Meet Melissa Coleman

When it comes to feeding a family, the kitchen can feel anything but simple. Bringing kids into the kitchen can be simultaneously daunting and rewarding. I feel passionately about cooking with kids; despite the challenges I believe it's worth the effort. I asked my friend Melissa Coleman to give us some advice on cooking with our kids. She is a mother, designer, and a fairly legendary home cook. She, her husband, and daughter live in Minneapolis, Minnesota. Melissa is the author of the book *The Minimalist Kitchen* and the founder of The Faux Martha website. Much like myself, she's passionate about cooking with kids.

So, I asked Melissa...

How can we get kids into the kitchen?

Here's how she answered:

I'll start by saying this—despite how painful it can be, it's important to bring kids into the kitchen, to teach them from an early age how to feed their bodies. How to choose the best variety of fuel to put in their car. It's a basic life skill that is often overlooked or put off as they're running out the door to college. There's good reason (and many reasons) it plays out this way.

To announce the obvious, it's hard to have kids in the kitchen. I've cried and yelled over spilled milk and splashed batter. I've said sorry, too. Many times. But, like all things tedious about parenting (sleep training, potty training, etc.), it gets better with time and comes with many benefits.

When trying to implement something new, like bringing kids into the kitchen, I've learned I do best when I take an honest look at the situation and when I consider the hard parts, too. So, let's do just that. Below is a quick list of reasons we keep kids OUT of the kitchen. *Out!*

- The mess—there's too much of that already.
- Time! Never enough time.
- This is *my* quiet time.
- Knives are sharp.
- The stove is hot.

From this list, we should just wait until they're heading out the door on their way to college to talk about cooking, if at all. If I didn't just watch my five-year-old decide, on her own, to save her almond butter stuffed chocolate cup for later because she was full, or watch her cut apples for applesauce, or watch her peel carrots for dinner (and steal a couple for herself), I wouldn't persevere. But I did witness all these wonderful moments. It still shocks me, too, that these tiny lessons I've been teaching her about the kitchen, about listening to her body, are slowly (did I mention slowly?) starting to sink in.

Let's start by addressing one of the biggest issues: our own lack of confidence in the kitchen. How do you begin to teach kitchen/eating skills when they

weren't taught to you? To begin with, I imagine you know more than you think. Just own that for a second. And then choose a handful of recipes. Start with twenty or so. And learn those recipes well. Notice the techniques you're using: boiling, simmering, steaming, roasting, chopping, dicing, slicing, mixing, stirring, folding. If you think you need to know everything before you start teaching, you don't! The best teachers are the best learners.

Here's a couple of simple tips for bringing kids into the kitchen:

- Play the long game on this one. Bring them into the kitchen when the recipe is right, when they can easily chop, peel, or stir. Don't feel they need to be in the kitchen every time you're in the kitchen. It can be your quiet space at the end of the day, too. Try starting with a couple of times a month, on a night or morning that feels less stressful. Two years later (or maybe sooner, but don't count on it), you'll begin to see the fruits of your labor.
- Give your kids age-appropriate tasks that will help them build confidence in the kitchen, not the opposite. I speak from experience here. I wanted to introduce my daughter to everything at once. It came from a place of excitement. But I found myself redirecting and getting frustrated with her too often. Once again, slow down and play the long game.
- Consider purchasing a set of nylon, serrated knives to protect tiny fingers but introduce the feeling of chopping. These knives are like training wheels for the big guys and will give you piece of mind when you turn your back to strain the boiling pasta. When switching over to the sharp knives, try taking a knife skills class together; a rite of passage.
- Use cooking as a way to talk about developmentally appropriate math and science skills. You can talk about everything from counting and adding to boiling point, fractions, and surface area.

PART TWO
THE SIMPLE APPROACH TO PARENTING

EXPANDING SIMPLICITY TO YOUR MINDSET

In Part One we learned how to clear our physical space and create a simple home that functions for the whole family. Now it is time to expand that simple philosophy to how we interact with our kids and our attitudes toward parenting. The two things are inextricably intertwined. You will see how having a clearer home will naturally move you toward a shift in your thinking and parenting. The guidance here is designed to open more space for an authentic and fulfilling family life, with less of the worry and clutter.

As parents, we have the best intentions. Happiness, health, and success are what we want the most for our children. But brace yourself as I deliver this unfortunate news: We can't give our kids any of that stuff. Happiness, health, and success isn't ours for the gifting. Our children are going to have to seek and discover those things for themselves.

But that doesn't stop us from trying. Those good intentions we harbor may manifest themselves in our parenting like this:

- Keeping our kids entertained constantly.
- Buying an excess of toys and clothes.
- Solving all their problems and managing their conflicts for them.
- Protecting them from all the risks, both physical and emotional.
- Pressuring them to be more.

These good intentions are exhausting. **They make parenthood heavy.** Much too heavy for most of us to handle. As a result, many of us are relying on coffee to wake us up and get us through the day, and cocktails to help us shut it all down at night to go to sleep.

We are overwhelmed and tired. We feel like no matter how hard we try in parenthood, we need to be more and we need to do more. As parents, we want to fix all their problems and prevent all their tears. When we spend all our time and energy trying to be superheroes our children miss out on opportunities to learn and grow. When we seek simplicity, we will find that less is more—even in parenting.

Like many mothers, I spent my first pregnancy idealizing what family life would be like. In my idealized image of family life, the home was always tidy. The baby was always perfect. The parents were always joyful. Our idealized family woke up every day smiling. We spent all our free time ogling each other, deeply in love. We took fabulous vacations with long walks on the beach and wrote our names in the sand. Perhaps most importantly, my idealized kids never, ever had crusted snotty noses.

But in real life, it doesn't seem so simple. You'll be deep in love, but you won't always be smiling. One of your kids will run through your sand writing before you can capture it for social media. And above all, I promise you this: No matter how often you wipe their noses, they are still going to be crusty.

Sometimes we see other parents who are measuring up. They are raising picture-perfect children. As I write this book in a Manhattan coffee shop, I just wrapped up a lovely conversation with a gentleman sitting nearby. Upon learning that I was writing a parenting book, he wanted to share a parenting success story: His niece, he tells me, is a college freshman studying pre-medicine. She is beautiful, kind, and ambitious. His nephew is a high school sophomore. He's exceptional in sports. He's a great looking kid with perfect hair.

My mind quickly wandered to the mother of these idyllic children. These children were clearly parented by June, the perfect mother we met in the introduction. Isn't that where perfect children come from, perfect parenting?

Yet despite what their Instagram photos lead you to believe: Good hair, athleticism, and medical school do not equate to happiness. Of course, if these are the things your children naturally excel in and that make them shine, fantastic. But as parents that choice is not ours for the making. We have to be willing to give up control and allow our children the space to find their own passions, ambitions, and ultimately their own path. Chasing perfection can have the tendency to feel empty, for parents and children alike.

You will never find happiness in the pursuit of perfection. But you will find it when you give up the chase. It is humbling to realize that despite all amounts of molding, prying, twisting, and pushing we will never be able to make our children into the idealized images that we have for them. Idealization in parenthood is dangerous. Life rarely takes the course that we expect or hope.

When we idealize, reality looks ugly. Our homes are never tidy enough, our children are never well-behaved enough, and our partners are never happy enough. We are never enough.

As parents, our days can often feel black or white. Once in a while you will feel a hint like June. You will get all the kids down for a simultaneous nap, get a workout in, and fix a healthy dinner. Those days you will feel like you are #winning. But most days won't be like that. Most days are *not* rainbows and butterflies. But you are not losing. You are not failing.

Parenthood isn't black or white.

Parenthood is meant to be gray. Sometimes you will in fact get a fluttering of rainbows and butterflies. Other times you will feel overcome with darkness. But most days are simply a beautifully imperfect, warm shade of gray.

Embrace the gray. Fall in love with the ordinary, regular, everyday moments and people that are right in front of you. Happiness, health, and success cannot be gifted to our children, but they are contagious. So start with *you*. Your intentions are good, but you can let up on the gas pedal. Because when it comes to raising children, less is more.

LESS FEAR

I let my kids wander a little, climb trees, and I don't stress if somebody skins a knee. I am letting my kids learn how to read when they are good and ready, rather than pushing it because the kid next door is doing it already.

My motto is that I kiss the boo-boos, but I don't prevent the falls.

That might sound crazy—why would any mother let her child get hurt? Here's why. Let's say I jump in and prevent that fall and so my child doesn't experience hurt. I am going to be doing the same thing again tomorrow. And the next day. And the day after that. Before you know it, my kid is twenty-two and I am still running around preventing boo-boos.

But if I let them fall they will learn how to stand back up. They will learn how to prevent themselves from falling again. Of course, I will be there along the way to offer kisses, bandages, and support. But I won't be the all-knowing protector of my child at any age, whether she is two or twenty-two.

We must not let fear rule our children's lives. We must not let our fear as parents rob them of valuable opportunities to grow and develop.

Sure, I appear pretty chill on the outside, but don't be fooled. There is a paralyzed, freaked-out mom living inside the shell of a calm woman. I am coming clean: I worry about my kids' safety and well-being. I worry about their education and future. I am terrified of losing them or failing to provide what they need. *Those fears are all very much alive inside of me.* Yet, I refuse to hover. I refuse to parent through the lens of fear. Because I know that my children are always learning and developing and I don't want to stand in the way of that process.

THE NORMALIZATION OF ANXIETY

By choosing to parent with less fear you will be in the minority. Parenting through fear has become not only socially acceptable, but it is socially expected. Being fearful and hovering is what "good" parents do.

When my daughter climbs to the top of the highest slide, strangers will call to her and tell her that she is going to fall.

She is *not* going to fall. **My daughter is capable.** She can do anything she puts her mind to. My daughter is capable of great things. In order for her to accomplish great things, she needs to have the confidence that she is capable. So, when it comes to our kids, let's stop perpetuating self-doubt and start conveying confidence.

As parents, we live in eternal fear for our children's safety and well-being. But let's call it like it is: Constant fear is better termed as anxiety. When fears linger beyond immediate threats and start to perpetuate your life in a more vague, diffused way, you are experiencing the emotion of anxiety.

I have anxiety. There's a very good chance that you do, too. Anxiety is an epidemic of modern parenthood and childhood. The National Institute of Mental Health indicates that 31.1 percent of adults in the United States experience an anxiety disorder at some point in their lives and 31.9 percent of children aged between thirteen and eighteen have had an anxiety disorder.

Anxiety can be a scary word for some. For the purposes of this book I will use the words fear, worry, and anxiety interchangeably. Being aware of my anxiety has been my best tool in helping to keep it under control. We have to take care of ourselves first so that we can properly take care of our children.

THE IMPACT ON OUR CHILDREN

While fear may in fact be one of the most primitive and vital sensations for the survival of humanity, it can be crippling for those who face it on a regular basis. When parents send the message that the world is a scary place, the fears may be passed onto the children. It is well recognized in research that anxiety runs in families. While there is some genetic basis for this, the type of environment that a child is reared in also impacts the anxiety and stress levels of the child. In short, parental anxiety can filter down to children making them more anxious as a result.

Studies also show that parental fear and hovering can be detrimental to the well-being of our kids. Persistent fear and anxiety in childhood can affect a young child's learning, development, and emotional well-being. When parents tirelessly hover over children, there can be a correlation with poorer emotional functioning, decision making, and academic performance[1]. These children, tend to struggle to manage their own emotions and behaviors as they grow into adolescence.

As parents we have the natural tendency to spend all of our energy trying to keep our children alive. In the process we forget to let them live. The reality is that children are very capable of managing basic risks and they learn confidence through risk-taking. As they grow we have to give them increasing amounts of space to safely let them wander, explore, take risks and challenge themselves.

We are positioned to provide guidance for our children as they grow. We are the primary role models for managing stress and overwhelm. While it is vital that, as parents, we are sensitive and responsive to the needs of our children, we still must allow ample opportunities for them to practice managing their emotions and behaviors independently of us.

We have to give them opportunities to mess up, fail, and make mistakes.

BRINGING AWARENESS TO YOUR FEARS

Teacher and journalist Elizabeth Stone wrote that "Making the decision to have children is momentous. It is to decide to forever have your heart go walking around outside your body." I was a worrier before I had kids. But now that my heart is walking around outside my body I feel an increasing need to

amp up my worrying. Post-kids, this natural inclination has led me to hover over my children's safety and well-being with every ounce of my energy.

As parents we experience two types of fear for our children: We fear for safety and for well-being. The first step in learning to parent with less fear, is to bring awareness to our anxieties and to understand where they stem from.

Safety fears

A generation ago, we received the news in the morning newspaper and the evening television broadcast. The only way we heard about kidnappings was on the milk carton. We knew that the world wasn't a perfectly safe place to live in, yet we were not bombarded with this reality twenty-four hours a day.

The increasing awareness of personal safety issues has led parents to a higher than necessary level of perceived risk. We feel like the world is a scarier place in the present day, despite the fact that the crime statistics tell us otherwise. The research shows that the world today is safer than in previous generations. Yet social media inundates us with friends of friends of friends who have experienced rare, yet devastating circumstances— childhood cancer, kidnappings, dry drowning, and an assortment of other vulnerabilities that we previously were less aware of have been brought to the forefront.

This constant awareness of safety risks through the news and social media breeds fear. And sometimes this fear can spiral out of control. Any bruise could mean cancer. Any innocent older gentleman may be a potential kidnapper. A few too many mouthfuls of water at the swimming pool may mean dry drowning.

As parents we need to be aware of our child's safety. The key is learning to distinguish between essential safeguarding—such as keeping an eye on our kids around open water—and exaggerated fears that cause us to hover unnecessarily or limit our children to satisfy our need to make sure they never experience even the smallest fall. Practice bringing awareness to your anxieties and questioning whether the decisions you are making are best for your child's safety, or simply pandering to your own anxiety.

Well-being fears

Our fears as parents are not only limited to safety. We also fear for the emotional, social, and physical well-being of our children.

We worry that if they don't have the right toys and clothes they will feel left out amongst their peers. We worry they will be bullied. We worry they may struggle at school. We worry that they won't eat enough. We worry they will eat too much.

In our desire to give our children happiness, health, and success we want to control all the external variables. We don't want them to suffer or experience hardships. **We want to protect their hearts just as much as their bodies.**

Social media has played a role in perpetuating this fear as well. Unbeknownst to us, we can fall into patterns of comparison. Your friend's child was speaking in full sentences when your kid could barely utter a "Ma-ma." Is there something wrong? Your cousin's son was writing his name in perfect form at three years old and your child still eats the crayons rather than coloring with them. Is he even going to get into college?

But as we have seen, there is no one route through childhood development, no one perfect path. Children are all wonderfully unique, they will do things at their own pace, they will excel in their own areas. They will have their own quirks and charms. These are the things that make them the characterful individuals that we love. So, let's allow them to flourish at their own pace rather than placing them in some invisible competition with their peers.

CHOOSE TO PARENT WITH LESS FEAR

The natural fears we all have for our children are not going to disappear overnight. But we have to intentionally rein it in and begin to filter it. Rather than acting on every impulse to protect our children, we need to *choose* to parent with less fear. We have to consciously choose to parent with less fear, because it won't come naturally for most of us.

Maybe you never wanted to be a lifeguard. But here you are, living life at the edge of the pool. This job as a parent requires you to make constant judgment calls: Who is really drowning versus who is simply learning how to swim?

As a lifeguard, you can't jump in every time a little swimmer goes underwater. Because if you do, you are going to quickly get exhausted and start drowning yourself. Instead, you need to keep a watchful eye on the pool. Most of the time, the little swimmer's head will go underwater and he will rather awkwardly paddle his way right back to the surface. He finds his way back because he is capable. But he's a new swimmer, so his technique looks a little messy and chaotic—it's kind of scary and hard to watch. But he prevails. He finds his way back to the top and tries again. Each time he's a bit more graceful and skilled.

If you jump in to save him each time he goes under, he won't get to practice swimming. And your actions are telling him that he shouldn't even try, because he's not capable without you.

Let's sit at the edge of the pool and make careful decisions: Is he really drowning or is he simply learning how to swim?

We have to slow down, observe, and learn how to tell the difference. We have to let them swim.

HOW TO PARENT
WITH LESS FEAR

☐ BREAK FROM THE NORM

Parenting through the lens of fear has become the social norm for our society. We expect parents to hover and prevent every fall. This is a heavy burden to carry and will leave us sinking instead of swimming.

☐ UNDERSTAND THE IMPACT

Not only is parenting with fear heavy for us, but it also has an impact on the development of our children. Our fears are contagious. Instead of perpetuating self-doubt, let's convey our confidence in our children through our actions and our words.

☐ BE AWARE

Every parent has fears for their child's safety and well-being. The first step in getting it under control is to become aware of it. Pay attention to where the fear is coming from and how it fuels your words and actions.

☐ CHOOSE LESS FEAR

For most of us, parenting with less fear won't come naturally. We have to actively choose to let our children mess up, fail, and make mistakes. Each time they stand back up they will be more graceful and skilled than the last.

How to use worry-batching

This is a mind trick. The mind responds better to redirection than it does extinction (which means to "extinguish" or stop a behavior). If you try to tell yourself to "stop worrying," it's like telling someone "don't think about a white elephant." Of course, you are going to think about a white elephant. **Therefore, instead of dismissing worry, we are going to acknowledge it and redirect it.**

Our minds have the tendency to wander and fall down into rabbit holes of worry. Becoming aware of our worries will allow us to address whether or not they are actually worthy of our time and energy. When we become aware of them, we can let them go.

Maybe you have heard of batching. It means to dedicate an amount of time to a certain area of interest or need. You might batch meals on Sunday by making them for the whole week. You can do the same with worries: batch your worries. Here's how: Set an alert on your phone or a block of time on your calendar each week. This is your set time and day to do all your worrying.

The goal is for you to recognize when you are worrying. **It's all about bringing it to your awareness.** When you catch yourself worrying throughout the week, remind yourself: "Oops, it's not time for worrying now—save this for batch time."

Here's the secret: **The vast majority of the time you will never use your batch time.** Because when batch time comes around you will be like...what was it I was worrying about again? Most of the worries will have come and gone by that time.

Mindfulness for kids

When children's emotions are running high—it's easy to start asking them to do things like "calm down" or "relax."

Our kids are doing the best that they can with the tools that they have available to them. There are two main reasons kids have a hard time keeping the big feelings under control.

1. Their frustration tolerance is naturally lower than that of an adult. This will increase gradually as their brains develop.

2. They have not yet been equipped with tools to find calm and quiet when they are feeling out of control.

It seems simple to request that they "calm down" or "relax." But most children just don't know how to do these things. With maturity they will begin to control their frustration, but in the meantime we can empower them with simple mindfulness practices. Here's my favorite technique.

The Mindful Hug

Give your child a big hug. With young toddlers and pre-schoolers it can be helpful to execute a laying down hug: Lay on your back and lay the child on top of you. For older children, a standing hug will accomplish the same.

During the long embrace take a few deep, slow, calculated breaths. Your child may naturally begin to replicate your breath by being in close physical contact with you. You can explain you are taking deep breaths to calm your body. Then, after a few quiet moments, invite your child to take three deep breaths with you while you count slowly. At any time, they are allowed to opt out or simply observe you.

The act of physically feeling your breath and your calm body can be transferred onto your child.

This doesn't work for every child in a moment of chaos. If your child prefers not to be touched while they are upset, invite them to practice The Mindful Hug during calm moments rather than chaotic ones.

LESS RUSH

I am a Fast Processor. That means my brain moves quickly and my body moves quickly to keep up with it. I walk fast. I talk fast. I think fast. I have the natural tendency to live on autopilot and do life in overdrive. On the plus side of this, I am goal-orientated and uber-productive. On the down side of this, although I reach my goals I also have the tendency to be careless and messy in the process.

I married a Slow Processor. He's a man who likes to do things slowly and methodically. When I send him to the grocery store, he has been known to take a half hour to pick out the right type of shredded cheese. He takes longer to get things done, but he does things right. He is neither careless nor messy.

It took me many years to appreciate this difference in our brains. If I had a dollar for every time I told him to "hurry up" in our relationship, I would be retired and living on the beach in Costa Rica.

We are blessed to be raising one of each: a Slow Processor *and* a Fast Processor. My son is careful and calculated. He always puts his trash in the garbage can and takes his plate to the sink. But sometimes he daydreams and takes twenty minutes to put on his shoes. My daughter simply tosses her garbage on the floor and leaves her plate on the table, but she will get her shoes on faster than you can say "we are going to the playground."

We all have the tendency to do life at different speeds. Our brains and bodies are wired differently. But one thing is for certain, society values fast.

There is so much peace to be found in less hurrying. As parents, it is easy to fall prey to this pressure and to fill up our calendars—and those of our kids—with a whirlwind of activities, social engagements, playdates, and trips. In a simple approach to parenting, the challenge is to step back from this and invite more time and space into our calendars. Once we do this, both the Fast Processors and the Slow Processors in the family—kids and parents alike—will benefit.

SOCIETY TELLS US THAT FASTER IS BETTER

"How are you doing?"

"Oh, I've been busy. Things have been crazy. Life is just so…you know, busy these days."

We are busy, and we continuously receive the message that busy is better. The world of today moves quickly. We are constantly in search of ways to multitask, to be more productive, and to do more. **But all this busyness comes at a cost. When we are doing everything, we aren't doing anything well.**

Because of the way my brain works, I easily fall into the trap of overcommitting, hurrying, and being physically present yet mentally absent. My body is here, but my brain is ten steps ahead. The problem is that I only ever knew one speed—and it just so happens that the speed I was moving at was the speed that society rewards. But it's also a speed that is synonymous with stress and overwhelm.

But I am not alone. The shift toward a fast-paced society is well underway. Stress-related disorders are on the rise and as a result we see increasing rates of health concerns such as obesity, depression, attention disorders, and learning disabilities. The epidemic of chronic overscheduling could be contributing to mood and behavior disorders in children and adults alike. It is important to recognize how chasing a fast-paced life can be detrimental to the well-being of us all.

STOP CHECKING OFF BOXES

When we are hurrying through life we become inclined to focus on speed and productivity. In other words, we pride ourselves on the number of boxes we can check on any given day. *There is no time to slow down. There is no time for lingering.*

Several years ago, my husband (then boyfriend) and I took our first trip together. We spent a week in Italy where we wined, dined, and hiked our way through Tuscany. It was my first international trip and it was exhilarating. For months I saved money and planned every aspect of our adventure in advance. I had it planned down to the hour: I wanted to make sure we used our time wisely, so we could do everything and see everything. I planned where we would eat, sleep, and explore. I knew exactly what the trip was going to look like before we even got on the plane.

Halfway through the trip, we set out on a (pre-planned) hike. It was gorgeous. But it was long. We had dinner reservations for which we needed to return. Yet my husband kept stopping us every few minutes to linger.

Finally, I had had enough. I said to him sharply, "It's just another view." Because to me it was just another view. I had already checked the box that said "see the view" and now I was ready to go. I was physically and mentally unable to linger. Frankly, at the time I had no desire to even try. It would be a decade before I realized that he was the one that had it all figured out.

Lingering isn't a deficit, it's an art. Lingering is the art of learning to slow down and appreciate exactly what's in front of you.

This is a particularly important skill to learn as a parent. Childhood can feel like an endless parade of checkboxes: first steps, check; first day at school, check; recorder recital, check; exam results, check; and so on, and so on. This not only puts undue pressure on our children to conform to "the schedule," but it also distracts us from the actual living and enjoyment of the many in-between moments of their precious childhood. No matter if we are natural fast or slow processors, we need to teach ourselves the art of lingering with our children rather than rushing them from one checkbox to the next.

LET GO OF THE "WHAT IFS"

In instances like our Italian holiday, I always told myself that I was a "planner" and that's just how planners operate. We make a schedule and we stick to it. But it would be years before I realized the truth. My desire to plan our lives out to the very last detail wasn't because I was a planner, it was because I had anxiety.

I had anxiety that looked like a serious case of the "What ifs."

- What if we miss our dinner reservation and we can't find anywhere to eat?
- What if we get lost and we end up taking the long way?
- What if my plan goes awry?

The "What ifs" never went away. In fact, after we had kids they came in strong.

- What if we can't afford a house in a good school district?
- What if she can't read before she goes to kindergarten?
- What if he gets bullied?

"What ifs" are a black hole that you will not emerge from. Regardless of how much time you spend pondering, planning, and researching for

your "What ifs," they will not disappear. They will simply be replaced with new ones.

Here's the tricky thing about the "What ifs"—they are almost always fruitless. We wind up spinning with fear and worry for the future and miss out on the people and opportunities present today. The time spent pondering, researching, and planning for them can drain us physically and emotionally. As when learning to parent with less fear, we need to take control of our anxieties to prevent them controlling us. Instead of focusing on the "what ifs," we need to practice living for today. That means being fully present with the life and love that's right in front of your nose.

Getting our anxiety under control is not easy: This simplicity thing is a journey. I still battle the "what ifs", but I am learning to let go. I am learning to live slow. I am scheduling less on our calendar. I am not checking off boxes and planning out every last detail of our future. I have no idea where or if my children will go to college or what their future careers will entail. But the view from this angle is beautiful. It's a striking shade of gray and I wouldn't have it any other way.

Take your foot off the gas pedal and put the car in neutral. Then start coasting so you can embrace the hills and valleys that your life will bring. Because you aren't going to want to miss this view.

CHOOSE TO PARENT WITHOUT RUSH

"The more slowly trees grow at first, the sounder they are at the core, and I think the same is true of human beings." —Henry David Thoreau

The speed we live life at will become an expectation for our children as they grow. When we are living life in high gear, it's only natural to bring our children along for the ride. And considering I have the tendency to do everything fast, I just assumed that my first child would do the same. He would walk early. He would talk early. He would check every box I laid out for him right on schedule.

He did no such thing.

When my son walked late, I felt like there was something I was doing wrong. I wanted to give him all my support and all the things. He had every type of shoe on the market and an equally large variety of walking devices to get him moving. I thought if I pushed him I could get him caught up with his peers.

When we have big plans for our kids, we have a lot of boxes to check. If they aren't checking those boxes fast enough, we fear that they will get left behind. We start pushing and pressuring them to be more and do more.

My son's friends were already running. He couldn't even stand up. How was he ever going to win at this race of life if he literally couldn't even stand up? Here's the kicker, *my son was fine*. Children grow on their own schedules. The truth was that I was the one who was not fine. I was the one in a race. In the process I was teaching him, but I wasn't teaching him how to walk, I was teaching him that he wasn't enough.

This hit me like a ton of bricks. If a child isn't good enough for his mother, how will he ever be good enough for himself? How would he ever learn to love himself for who he is, if his mother wasn't content to do that very thing?

Remember, parenting is not always easy, we will experience moments of darkness. Realizing this truth was part of my darkness.

I made a choice to stop living ten steps ahead and start living in the right now. That's when I realized that he was teaching me too. I stopped checking off boxes. I withdrew him from the race. I fell in love with the exact person who was present in front of me at that very moment. Because I didn't need to fix him, I needed to fix me.

By choosing to parent with less fear we bring mindfulness to how our own anxieties about safety and well-being might be limiting our children from learning independence and realizing their own capabilities. Choosing to parent with less rush challenges us to tackle similar anxieties about developmental stages. By recognizing that our children grow at their own pace and divorcing ourselves from the modern comparison society, we will be better able to appreciate family life in all its fullness— and our children will be given the space to thrive.

HOW TO PARENT
WITH LESS RUSH

☐ BREAK FROM "FASTER IS BETTER"

In the world we live in we are constantly told that faster is better. Busy is seen as important. We often jump into the race without any idea of where it's taking us. The reality is that this type of lifestyle is synonymous with stress and overwhelm for both children and adults alike.

☐ STOP CHECKING OFF BOXES

A harried life will lead us to focus on checking off boxes and racing toward the next goal. But our children grow up too fast for this type of approach. We need to slow down and linger with them. Stop, breathe, and let your to-do list go. Soak up the view because it will be gone before you know it.

☐ LET GO OF THE "WHAT IFS"

"What ifs" are a deep black hole. Once you start wondering "what if" you will get sucked into a spiral that leads you to endless pondering, planning, and researching. Instead of living life ten steps ahead, live the best life you have today.

☐ CHOOSE TO PARENT WITHOUT RUSH

If we let it, society will lead us to a life of stress and overwhelm. As a result, we have to make lifestyle choices that will protect the social and emotional well-being of our children. We have to choose to let our children live slowly. Simplicity won't just happen to us, we have to choose it.

Three reasons to get outside

The world is so busy that nature can seem like an elusive place that takes great effort to visit. You might feel like you only need a big dose yearly when you get out to a State Park. Yet as humans we need to get outdoors every day—even if it's just a walk in the city or a cup of coffee on the porch. *It's nature and it counts.*

Childhood disorders are on the rise: ADHD, autism spectrum disorders, anxiety, depression—we have seen increasing rates across the board. The verdict is out on whether the lack of nature in this generation is correlated with the rise of such disorders, but what the research does show us is that all children will benefit from time spent in nature. Here are three reasons to get outside:

1. The brain needs it

When we send children outdoors their brains are stimulated. When kids are outside the sensory system experiences varied input, such as cold snow, wet rain, loud cracks of thunder, bright sun, and brisk wind. Children who spend all their time indoors are deprived of this significant sensory input. The sensations experienced in nature are important for development.

2. The body needs it

The body and brain are connected in infinite ways. We know that children need to be moving to learn. When they go outside, they are moving in unique, unstructured ways: climbing, balancing, lifting, etc. Similarly, with the rising obesity epidemic in mind, research shows us that this type of outdoor free play actually burns more energy than structured activities such as sports.

3. The Earth needs it

The countries in Scandinavia have the highest rates of sustainability efforts in the world. Residents of these countries respect and take care of the Earth so well that it almost seems like they have been brainwashed. What's the secret? They start them young. Scandinavian countries have ingrained the importance of nature into the mindsets of residents since birth. The babies nap outside and the children play outside. They learn to take care of the Earth because they have been born and bred to appreciate it.

LESS DISTRACTION

If only I could see June's social media profile, I imagine it would include a whole lot of photos of her playing with her kids. Like, *really playing.* She would be inventing games, engaging with educational toys, and rolling around on the floor with them. June probably also has a broad repertoire of arts and crafts activities on hand that her kids execute beautifully. She also takes them on daily nature walks that include lectures on tree identification.

Because she's perfect. And perfect moms provide all these things for their children, right?

Wrong. We are parents, not entertainers.

Sometimes as parents we think it's our job to fill in all the white space on the calendar. We fear that if we don't provide structured activities our kid will get bored. We fear that if we don't have a lot of toys they will be joyless. We fear that if our kid isn't highly scheduled their resumé, education, and future chance at success may be shortchanged.

But the truth is, boredom is a blessing. Letting our kids reclaim their white space is beneficial for their learning and development.

BOREDOM IS A GIFT

The same fears and anxieties that we have been looking at in the first two sections of this chapter, drive us to occupy our children all the time. We fear that otherwise we will be marked out as "bad parents", denying our children stimulation and holding them back from checking off those all-important

boxes. When we start to entertain our children, they come to expect entertainment. We fear boredom and through our constant efforts to prevent boredom, our children learn to loathe it even more.

But boredom is actually a special gift. It's just wrapped in a package that can be a little tricky to open up. When they get it opened up the real magic happens, because **boredom is simply a transitional phase that leads to deeper learning and development.**

Yet listening to kids complain about boredom is not easy. Not only does it hurt our ears, but it also causes self-doubt. This occurs because we interpret a bored child as an unhappy child. As parents, we never want our children to be unhappy.

Despite this, we need to give our children more white space to be bored. This white space will bring about the development of the skills needed to succeed in the world of tomorrow. This is because boredom leads to two important activities for learning in young children: imitation and unstructured play. These two elements provide the foundation for the skills needed for success in the next generation: critical thinking, collaboration, communication, and creativity.

First, let's start by discussing how young children learn. Then we'll talk about what they really need to know to be prepared for life.

UNDERSTAND HOW CHILDREN LEARN

When we think about young children learning and growing, we might have a mental image of a small person sitting at a desk. They might be cutting and pasting shapes and tracing letters. Sure, those things are great. But when it comes to our work as parents, the best thing we can do is to allow white space in our days so that our children can imitate skills seen in everyday life and engage in heaps of unstructured play.

Imitation of daily life

We are our child's first teacher and they are learning from us constantly. In addition to reading books aloud, we know that children learn best through modeling and incidental learning. Yet when we are doing mundane tasks like folding laundry, we often feel the need to occupy our children with something more "fun" or "kid-friendly." The truth is, they are better off standing next to us naturally learning through our world.

As parents we can breathe easier knowing that much of the early learning is self-directed and naturally occurring. We don't have to sit down and teach a lesson about where the body parts are located, nor do we need to show them a television show that explains this. This is because children learn the body parts through everyday interactions with us: Like when we talk to them in the bath tub and when they are getting dressed. They are learning every minute of the day through watching and imitating the life around them. We can have our kids by our side for both the exciting and the dull parts of life—because they are observing it all and soaking it up.

Therefore, make children part of the regular, typical rhythms of the home. That means, let them fold the washcloths, let them play in the bubbles while you wash the dishes, and take them to the grocery store. Children crave simple connection with adults and they do their best learning through watching and imitating everything that we do.

Unstructured play

Never underestimate the value of unstructured play, sometimes called pretend play or free play. In today's generation we have a tendency to lean toward highly structured activities rather than providing opportunities for kids to play freely. Unstructured play among children provides opportunities to practice conflict management, problem solving, and innovation.

Pretend play also provides opportunities for children to tell stories, which is an important pre-literacy skill. Free play allows kids to turn simple blankets

into forts, or cardboard boxes into spaceships to travel across the universe. This type of play gives children a window into make-believe worlds that we can't even imagine.

And imagination is important, because we live in an era of innovation. Did you know that most of your children will have careers that haven't even been invented yet?

Although unstructured play might seem like the opposite of structured academic work and formal education, it is actually the foundation for it. **Let's let our kids play.**

WHAT CHILDREN NEED TO LEARN NOW

Now that we have discussed the ideal ways for learning in the early years, let's talk about what our kids are learning through imitating life at home and free play.

The US-based organization, Partnership for 21st Century Skills, has identified the 4Cs—critical thinking, collaboration, communication, and creativity—to help shift education toward the needs of the future. A generation ago, a primary focus on learning and development was to teach our children content. This means things like:

- What year did World War II begin?
- What is the name of this insect?
- Who was the 23rd President of the United States of America?

At that time, we needed to memorize more content because it was difficult to acquire the facts. To gather facts we needed to jump in our car, drive to the library, and search out a book for the answer. These days, we just pick up our phones and Google it.

The way that we acquire knowledge has shifted dramatically. As a result, the way we educate our children needs to change too.

While content is still relevant and important to know, there are other areas of our children's education that need to be developed further to be effective in the next generation. Our children aren't going to simply need to memorize and regurgitate information. They are going to need to take that information and think critically, create, communicate, and collaborate.

The best part of this shift? It doesn't require a lot of extra work on our part. Children are actively practicing all these things in the comfort of their own homes by observing and imitating daily life and engaging in lots of unstructured play.

Critical thinking

As a generation that has a plethora of information at their fingertips, our children are going to need to be prepared with how to use it. That means we can't answer all their questions for them, instead we have to give them opportunities to search for the answers themselves. *They are becoming questioners as well as information seekers.*

Creativity

When our children have less entertainment, they will create more. Fewer toys will help foster imagination as they have to innovate new ways to use simple objects. When parents opt out of playtime, children will start writing the storylines. *They are becoming innovators as well as creators.*

Communication

Most children don't need to be directly taught communication, because they are practicing it in real-life interactions every day. When they are playing imaginatively, they practice new vocabulary and storytelling. They will become experts at listening and filtering the important information. *They are becoming listeners as well as talkers.*

Collaboration

When children are learning to work together, it can be awkward. They are not always polite, and they rarely agree. But when possible, allowing kids the time to practice teamwork and solve problems without adult intervention will empower them to be strong collaborators. *They are becoming team players as well as problem-solvers.*

CHOOSE TO PARENT WITH LESS DISTRACTION

As humans, we have the habit of taking the path of least resistance. Sometimes we call this going with the flow, or "the law of least effort." It means we choose the easy route when possible. As a result, most children will welcome easy entertainment like television or pre-planned activities. Unstructured play and imitation of daily life can be a lot of work—because it requires equal effort from the brain, body, and heart.

But remember, it's not our job to entertain. By providing our children with highly structured days, we are not doing our children any favors. It's our duty as parents to let our children fill in their own white space—because that's where the real magic happens.

HOW TO PARENT WITH LESS DISTRACTION

☐ EMBRACE BOREDOM

As parents, we have the tendency to avoid boredom like the plague. We feel the need to entertain our children. We believe that our efforts will improve their learning and development. But boredom is just a transition. Once our children learn how to push through boredom, they will begin to grow and develop in new ways.

☐ UNDERSTAND HOW CHILDREN LEARN

Young children learn in two ways: through imitating the life they see around them and engaging in unstructured play. That means, skipping the screen time and having them stir the pot while you are cooking instead. Consider opting out of soccer this season in favor of more time to play freely outside.

☐ WHAT A CHILD REALLY NEEDS

We are growing children, not building resumés. The children of today need opportunities to practice critical thinking, communication, creativity, and collaboration. The best part is that these things can all be done at home, in the white space that we choose to give them.

☐ CHOOSE TO PARENT WITH LESS DISTRACTION

Choosing to let our kids be bored is far from lazy, it's one of the most intentional strategies there is for raising kids to innovate and solve problems. Let us choose to stop filling up all the white space with structured activities and screen time. Instead, let's let them work through the transition of boredom and get back to the basics of being a kid.

Five tips to encourage free play

Nearly all children have the essential skills for play built inside of them. However, if they aren't used to playing freely then they may need some time and help to get back to the basics. Here are five tips to encourage unstructured play in young children:

1. **Have fewer toys.** When children have fewer toys, they are forced to find ways to create, imagine, and innovate with the toys that they have. *Less really is more.*

2. **Let them be bored.** The early stages of boredom can be whiny and painful for both the adult and child, but boredom is merely a transition that occurs before free play comes to fruition. *Ride it out.*

3. **Take them outside.** It's not always easy to get kids outside, but it opens doors to adventures and play that can't be replicated inside. *Find room for them to roam.*

4. **Give them simple prompts.** If your child is struggling to get involved with pretend play, give them simple prompts to get started. Suggest that a pile of blocks could be turned into a castle and let them take it from there. *You don't have to be the constant play companion, but you can help them get started.*

5. **Cut back on screen time.** When children get bored, they often lean on screen time. When we cut back on screen time they will find their way back to play. *Trust that play is what their bodies need, not screens.*

Getting screen time under control

Screen time is a hotly contested issue in the parenting community. Frankly, my kids can never get enough. Particularly my son, who spent the larger part of his first few years begging for it. In fact, one of his first sentences was "Curious George...five more minutes?"

I know that my kids really love screen time, but I don't love giving it to them. This is because I know that they need to be moving, and playing, and observing real life nearly constantly in the early years for health and development. **This means less time sitting in zombie mode and more time spent active and engaged.**

Here are two tips for getting screen time under control:

1. Explain it

I don't just tell my children "no" to requests for excessive amounts of screen time, instead I explain it. Giving a solid explanation turns it from a power struggle into me just "doing my job."

Here's how I say it: "It's my job as your Mama to make sure that your brain and body are healthy. For your brain and body to be healthy, they need lots of playing and moving. When you watch television, your brain and body aren't getting the exercise they need."

By explaining our decision to our children, we involve them in that decision-making process. Reducing screen time becomes a reasonable, understandable action rather than a punishment.

2. Schedule it

We have found that scheduling screen time each day nearly eliminates the begging. My kids don't have to ask when they will get it, because they know. Each day right after lunch they get forty minutes of TV time.

As parents, if you don't schedule screen time, you may often find yourself using it when you are overwhelmed and need a break. Usually because the kids are driving you crazy. When kids are full of energy, pushing our buttons, that's usually a sign that they need to expend energy in active play—preferably outdoors. If they get screen time under these circumstances, they *will* sit still and be quiet, but when that time is over that energy may be compounded and result in emotions running even higher.

Meet Nicole Kavanaugh

Outdoor play seems like the most natural play that there is. But for our current generation it's not always easy to get our kids outdoors. The amount of time that kids are spending outdoors is decreasing and the amount of time children are on electronic devices is increasing. This lack of time spent in nature is putting our children at risk for physical and mental health concerns—but there is hope. Getting children outdoors will require some time and effort on the part of the parent, but the effort is worth the reward.

My friend Nicole Kavanaugh is going to offer some helpful tips for taking children's play outdoors. Nicole is an advocate for child-led learning and the Montessori philosophy. She lives in Minnesota with her husband and three children—where they play outside regardless of the weather. She's the founder of the Kavanaugh Report where she brings insight on child-led education to parents around the world.

So, I asked Nicole...

How can we get kids outside?

Here's how she answered:

For so many parents, bringing their kids outside to play does not necessarily come naturally to them. But it is so important that we help to foster a connection between our children and the outdoors. Not only are there numerous physical and mental health benefits, time spent outdoors can bring a family closer together, it can foster curiosity and scientific discovery by your children, and create hours of creative play. Nature has the power to transform relationships. Siblings that are different ages, have different skill levels, and different interests can suddenly find common ground. Parents and children can connect over new discoveries and shared experiences.

Now, that sounds like a tall order, but this doesn't have to be an intimidating process. In fact, outdoor play is often enhanced by keeping it simple and going back to the basics. If you peruse any toy store, you'll find a variety of toys promising to entertain your child while outside. Most aren't necessary, and some can even take away from your time outdoors.

So, what can you do to foster creative and meaningful play outdoors? The first place to start is preparing your outdoor space for play. Take a look at your outdoor space from your child's perspective. Take stock of the things your child has available and think deeply think about how often you are giving your child access to these opportunities. Time in the outdoors is the cheapest, but sometimes the hardest, resource to give to our children. We have to give our children ample time in nature, so they can feel comfortable with the outdoors. Once comfortable, children can take ownership over their play. They can flex their creative muscles to grow and explore.

As you prepare your space, think about the things that your child likes to do. Is it hauling? Is it climbing? Is it painting? Then, make those opportunities available through your contact with the outdoors. This can be done by making changes to your own space or by visiting natural resources in your area. Create opportunities that speak to your child's individual interests and abilities. Let's say, for example, your child likes art. You could invite your child to create

something from natural materials gathered in the yard. This could be a mosaic created from collected rocks, or patterns made from sticks.

Another thing you can do to foster creative outdoor play is to prepare your child. It's best not to send children outside cold and hungry. Make sure they have the appropriate clothes for exploration. The last thing you want to stop your child from exploring the outdoors is that fancy outfit that you are worried about getting ruined—and the same thing goes for you! A well-fed, comfortable child will be much more inclined to explore, play, and grow in their relationship with the outdoors.

Finally, the most important thing you can do to foster creative outdoor play is to bring your own sense of wonder to the outdoors. Stand in awe with your child over all of the beautiful details you can find even in your own neighborhood. Let your child take the lead and ask questions. Then, just sit with those questions. Ponder why the leaves turn colors in the fall, or how birds fly. See the extraordinary in all the normal around you. Wonder with your child and see where that takes you.

LESS REFEREE

When I reflect back, life with one child was pretty peaceful. I had a beautiful twenty-seven months with my first child before I gave birth to my second. At the time of her birth, I thought I was just giving birth to one new creature. But much to my surprise, along with this child came another brand-new entity for whom I wasn't entirely prepared.

That third and new entity is the sibling relationship. For the purposes of this book, we are going to give that relationship a name: Meet Fuego.

Let me tell you a little bit about Fuego: He got his name because, well, he's often *en fuego* or "on fire." Fuego is a handful because he has primitive socialization and reasoning skills. He is completely undeveloped, a true work-in-progress, if you will. As a result, Fuego doesn't quite buy into the idea of sharing and pretty much always thinks everything belongs to him. Sometimes Fuego simmers quietly and provides warmth and comfort. But often he's roaring and explosive. Most days, he's my greatest obstacle. The hardest part of having Fuego living in our home is that he isn't mine. I can't control him and I can't manage him.

He wholly belongs to my son and my daughter.

Fuego is usually messy and irritating, but when he's good he is the most beautiful thing I have ever seen. This gives me hope because I have a lot of visions for what I want him to look like. I know exactly how I want him to behave. I want him to be kind and generous. I want him to be proud and loyal.

If I could just grab Fuego and fix him, I would do it in a heartbeat. But here's the thing, Fuego has a purpose. He's a practice ground for my children's future relationships. He is teaching them everything about conflict resolution, problem-solving, and negotiation. For this, I am thankful that he exists in my home—so they can learn these important things in a space that is safe to make mistakes.

You won't want to hear this, but it can take years for Fuegos to mature—whether between siblings, cousins, or friends. Sometimes it can take decades. I have heard of Fuegos who were just starting to hit their stride after twenty or thirty years. As much as I would like to hurry up the process and create peace and quiet in my home, I know that much of Fuego's development is out of my hands.

Even though he's a wildcard right now, I know that he is going to grow into something wonderful.

BE A COACH, NOT A REFEREE

Because the relationship between my children isn't mine, I can't call the shots. I can't referee. In spite of this fact, I am still standing on the sidelines and there are a few things I can do to help coach.

I have to constantly remind myself that I can't solve all my children's battles. Therefore, I won't rob them of the opportunity to practice doing it for themselves. So much of learning how to socialize is formed through real-life practice. This means when they argue among themselves, I let them work it out as much as possible.

When children practice social skills, they are learning how to communicate, how to listen, how to negotiate, and how to forgive. These are things we can't teach from a book. They are concepts that can't be retained through a lecture. Much of refining these skills comes from abundant opportunities to mess them up.

This often requires that we give our children physical space to interact with one another. When I know it's safe, I try to walk away and let my son and daughter interact without my constant watchful eye. If I am present and feel a confrontation brewing, I suddenly remember that I left my coffee in the other room and leave to retrieve it. Often the resolve will come before I can even find my mug.

Be warned, these self-made resolutions are awkward and sometimes ungraceful. They aren't always polite. They aren't always calm. But they are a work in progress and shouldn't be punished or ridiculed. Instead of telling them how *not* to handle conflict, we are going to work to teach them better ways through modeling good behavior ourselves and role-playing.

SAFETY FIRST

Allowing our children to work it out themselves assumes that there are no safety risks. That means that the physical space is safe and that the children aren't at risk of hurting one another. When these things aren't guaranteed we need to stay close and give them the amount of space that is comfortable for all involved.

BE A ROLE MODEL

If we want to empower our children to solve their own problems, first, we need to give them the space to practice, and second, we need to give them role models from which to learn. We know that children learn through imitation. This means that much of their early lives will be spent replicating and taking on behaviors that they learn from the people around them.

Pay attention to our modeling

We are the first teachers. They learn by watching us: husband–wife; parent–child; sister–brother. The good, the bad, and the ugly. That means we need to do our best to take care of our own relationships. Whether it's our marriage, or the dynamic with our own mother—our children are watching the ways that we handle conflict and resolution. Although we don't need to strive for perfection, we do need to strive to model the types of relationships that we want our children to replicate in their future.

But remember, you could be Mary Poppins and your children are still going to bicker. Regardless of how well you model good relational skills, your children are a work in progress. Social skills build slowly over the period of a lifetime. Trust that while your children are growing they are learning a solid foundation from you, even if they haven't perfected the art of peaceful human interactions just yet.

Try role-playing

We know that our children are always watching us and learning. They learn the foundation of their social skills from the people whom they are the most intimately connected to. As they are learning they can also get frustrated.

It's easy to get frustrated when you ask kindly for a friend to share a toy and you are met with a "no." This frustration can quickly turn into primitive caveman-like behavior, such as yelling, toy snatching, or even hitting.

Although we can't always predict or direct our children in the best way to respond to conflict, we can practice acting out scenarios through role-playing. In role-playing, you pretend play: Assume the role of the other child and practice using new language and non-verbal communication strategies. Here are three key points that we can practice and teach:

- Give other children physical space when they appear to be upset.
- Practice specific words that will clearly tell others when you don't like a behavior.
- Know when to seek support from adults.

ENABLE EXPANSION AND CONTRACTION

The thing about intimate relationships is that they are intense. The people we love the most are the people that fire us up the hottest. I find that occasionally I will still argue with my mother with the intensity and social skills of sixteen-year-old-me. The close nature of intimate relationships makes them all the more challenging to manage.

This goes for both children and adults.

You will notice that the most difficult relationships for your children to manage are the ones that mean the most to them: siblings, cousins, neighbors, and dear friends. This is because these intimate relationships take the form of Fuego—they are a safe practice ground to try out problem-solving and conflict management. In case you're wondering why they "never act this way at school"—there's your reason: Intimate relationships are the safe space to act a little crazy.

We can't fix or change these growing relationships but allowing them to expand and contract can be a powerful way to manage them. I first learned about this concept from Lawrence Williams in *The Heart of Learning*. Williams explains that when we expand, we move apart and operate independently. This means our kids are running outside and playing freely. When we contract, we are coming together and interacting in both a physically and emotionally close space. This might mean that we are doing a puzzle, making a LEGO creation, or reading a book.

Our kids cycle back and forth between expansion and contraction all day long. As parents, we can start to notice when they need to make the switch and help facilitate that. If they have been sitting at a table stacking blocks together for twenty minutes and all of a sudden they start elbowing each other—maybe it's time to expand. That means the blocks get put aside and the kids either go run outside or find play opportunities in separate spaces.

This isn't punitive. We aren't putting children into their rooms if they don't play nicely. We are simply giving them the space to breathe when they need it and cuing them to come back together when the time is right.

CHOOSE TO PARENT WITH LESS REFEREEING

It is hard to watch our kids struggle. Our nature as parents is to jump in to solve all their problems for them. That means we have to make the conscious choice to step back and let these relationships unfold naturally.

I love to watch my children solve problems and work through disagreements together. It rarely all comes together the way I hope, but it comes together nonetheless. This too shall pass, I remind myself in the face of each battle. My nose has other business in which to attend. With each breath of calm air I breathe into my own relationships, I can feel more confident that there are beautiful things ahead for my children.

HOW TO PARENT WITH LESS REFEREEING

☐ BE A COACH, NOT A REFEREE

As parents, we desperately want our kids to get along. As a result, we can spend a great deal of time managing their interpersonal relationships. The reality is that our kids need that practice ground to learn how to do it for themselves.

☐ BE A ROLE MODEL

Watching kids sort through challenges together can be hard, but it's important that we stand by to help coach rather than dictating the resolution. Our best tools to help our kids is to model positive relationships ourselves and to practice simple role-modeling with them.

☐ ENABLE EXPANSION AND CONTRACTION

The nature of intimate relationships is that they are intense. As parents we can help to recognize when our children need time to expand or have space to separate. Cuing our children to take some time apart shouldn't be punitive, but instead it should be built into the natural rhythms of their days.

☐ CHOOSE TO PARENT WITH LESS REFEREEING

When we want our kids to be happy, it can be easy to fall into the habit of fighting their battles for them. As a result, we have to choose to step back and let them practice working through challenges with their peers and siblings themselves.

What is intentional parenting?

When we parent with intention, we think before we act. We prioritize building a relationship with our kids over getting them to eat those last three bites of broccoli. Intentional parenting is about focusing on the big picture rather than getting caught up in all the tiny details. We are striving to be thoughtful and choose our battles wisely.

As parents, we put a lot of pressure on ourselves to be "good" parents. But sometimes that's exhausting. My husband has made the analogy that good parenting is like exercise—even if we know how to do it and we know the health benefits...we don't always feel like doing it. Sometimes we just want to sit on the sofa and eat cake rather than exercising, right? We all struggle with consistency. We are human. This means that you aren't always going to do and say the right things. You are going to get frustrated and yell at your kids. But you are the best person for the job. As parents, we are blessed by the fact that young children are immensely forgiving.

If intentional parenting is like exercise, then warmth and connection are the core work. The core is the center of your body and it needs to be strong and stable before you can build up the rest of your muscles. If your core is weak, you will struggle to have balance in other areas.

In intentional parenting, we build our core through a strong bond with our children. That bond is the path that we use to teach and guide our children. The foundation of that bond is warmth and connection.

Aim for warmth and connection in both the good moments and in the bad moments. When you have a strong core, you will always have that stability to ground your relationship with your kids. That bond will help their feet stay firmly planted on the ground.

Here are three of my favorite simple ways to build warmth and connection with kids:

- Get down at kid-level if possible, even though it hurts your knees
- Offer eye contact, even when they choose to look away
- Show them respect, even if it's hard to put your ego aside

Build your core just a little bit each day. This foundation will be the bond that brings respect and positive behavior that lasts a lifetime.

Meet Eloise Rickman

Parenthood and family life have the reputation of being chaotic. But it doesn't have to be so—especially when parents are tending to their own personal needs as well as the needs of their children. Eloise Rickman is a testament to the fact that peace and calm are very tangible principles to aspire toward with young children. She and her husband reside in a sunny house full of books in London, England, where she works as a writer and parent educator. Eloise is the founder of Frida Be Mighty, where she advocates and teaches a peaceful parenting approach.

So, I asked Eloise...

Why is self-care important in parenthood?

Here's how she answered:

It is often assumed that if you are to be a good parent, then you must sacrifice your needs for those of your children, pushing aside your interests and desires. I disagree. In fact, I think it's pretty much impossible to be a gentle, joyful, and connected parent if you don't prioritize your own self-care.

It is much harder to be patient and stay calm with your children when you are exhausted.

It is much harder to nourish your child's intellect when you're not looking after your own.

It is much harder to show your children what a healthy, happy adult looks like when you are burnt out.

It is much harder to model self-worth when your actions show that you do not see yourself as worthy of being taken care of.

The idea that when you become a parent your needs are erased is one that is far reaching and contributes to so much unnecessary guilt, and I'm sure contributes to our high rates of postpartum depression in the West. We know from solid research that having good support and self-care in place is one of the best protections parents can have against depression and anxiety. Prioritizing self-care is not just a gift to yourself as a parent, but a gift for your whole family. Think of yourself as an instrument—when you take time to tune yourself, the music you play is so much sweeter.

Of course, there are seasons in life when finding space for self-care is truly hard. But even in these moments, it's still possible to find simple ways to nurture yourself. Self-care doesn't always mean time away from your children. You can still be around your kids and take moments to put your own needs first—and even better, you can find creative ways to meet your own needs while meeting your children's needs, too. Self-care will look different for everyone; for you it might be a walk in the woods with your children, a coffee

alone in the early morning sunshine, reading poetry aloud as a family, or a hot bath before bed.

If the idea of carving out time for self-care feels overwhelming right now, start small. Focus on slowing down your breath and counting each one in and out until you get to twenty. Take five minutes whilst your children are playing to make a hot drink, and drink it without doing anything else. Plan your journey so that you arrive at school pick-up a few minutes early, and spend that time reading a few pages of a good book.

Parenting can be a truly radical act. The way in which we raise our children can have a profoundly positive impact not just on our families but on our communities and our world. Creating a family dynamic where simplicity, connection, empathy, and kindness are at the heart of the home can be life changing. But this takes work, and this work is much harder when we are not taking care of ourselves.

Just remember: Self-care is not selfish. Looking after yourself allows you to better look after your children, nurture your relationships, serve those around you, and show up in the world as the human you truly want to be.

LESS STUFF

The excitement on a child's face when they receive a gift is priceless. But when that joy comes from material things, it is fleeting. The excitement lasts minutes, or hours at best. That's because it's actually a quick rush of neurochemicals in our brains, such as dopamine, serotonin, and oxytocin. This brief type of excitement (or surge of chemicals) feels good, but it leaves us craving the next rush.

This goes for the gift-giver too. We get the same excitement. It feels good to give our kids stuff, so we keep doing it. We keep buying and we keep accumulating it.

But what if we taught our children to seek out joy and excitement that doesn't involve "stuff?" Instead, let's show them enduring joy that comes from the real gifts: love, life, and adventure. I want my children to seek excitement through new life experiences. I want them to seek joy through loving relationships.

FOCUS ON THE REAL GIFTS

Keeping children focused on the real gifts is hard work. I recently returned from a work trip where I was away from my children. On route home I was at the train station and passed a window display with a stuffed animal that my daughter would adore. My instant thought was—what a nice surprise this would be to bring her a thoughtful gift after being away. I imagined her face lighting up and the surge of joy it would bring us both.

But I took a pause and reflected on this thought. I have to check myself and examine my inclinations because "simple and intentional" living isn't yet ingrained into my bones. After years of simplifying, I still find myself caught up on the excitement of buying my kids things that will make them smile.

There is no harm in sweet, little *thoughtful* surprises, but I made the choice to opt out of a tangible gift on this occasion. I did it because I need to be intentional about the quantity and quality of items that I bring into my home. But I also need to be intentional about the relationship that I am facilitating between my children and stuff. I had been traveling and upon returning home the gift is *me*. The gift is my presence, my hugs, and my time. **I don't want my children to take any of that for granted.** I don't want them to be distracted from the joy that the gift of our relationships brings. I don't want them to grab my suitcase and start looking for a package while barely giving me a passing glance.

I want my children to focus on the real gifts: Love, life and, adventure. If we seek our joy in these true gifts, our children will follow suit. But the "stuff" can be so distracting. It's hard to get excited about birthday guests when you have a table full of wrapped birthday gifts waiting for you. It's hard to focus on welcoming your father home from a work trip when there's a Transformer waiting in his suitcase. It can be hard to focus on the new sibling you are meeting in the hospital when you have an American Girl doll hiding under wrapping paper next to the bed.

The ways that we give will teach. Let's choose to give love over stuff, because it is enough.

IT STARTS WITH YOU

As a teenager, my friends and I spent our weekends hanging out at the shopping mall. I grew up in a small town that didn't have much in the way of entertainment. The mall was the place that we passed the time. When we had money, we would buy stuff. But most of the time, we would just linger amongst the stuff and wish we could own more of it.

I always thought that was the goal: Study hard, go to college, get a good job, make lots of money, buy lots of stuff. Those are the rules, right?

Society and the media perpetuate this idea that "the stuff" is what will make us happy. As a result, our sense of self-worth gets wrapped up in the search for the stuff. Our love and lives get wrapped up in our stuff, too. But we don't wear our worth on our bodies. We don't drive our worth. And the house we live in does not display our worth. Your worth is far more than anything you can purchase.

We get to make choices. And as parents, it starts with us: We are steering the ship.

We go after the good job and try to make lots of money. We keep working harder because we keep seeking more. **Yet the irony in that is that the seeking is actually disruptive to the search for the real gifts.** When it comes to joy, the stuff will keep us seeking those brief surges of chemicals. But the stuff will always fall short on bringing the real gifts. Because the more you seek the stuff, the more elusive life and love become.

Living outside of New York City, I see this every day. Individuals that commute four hours per day to make money at a job they hate to pay for a beautiful house that they rarely get to enjoy. But that's what we do because that's how society tells us we are supposed to live. Those are the rules that society has laid out for us: **Study hard, go to college, get a good job, make lots of money, buy lots of stuff. Then do life bigger, better, faster, and busier.**

Of course, we all need to make ends meet, and sometimes that means putting the hours in. As much as having too much stuff can distract from the real gifts in life, having too little is a real struggle. The challenge with this first-world problem is when we are in the privileged position of having enough—we rarely know when to draw the line. We can struggle to make a conscious decision about our levels of consumption as parents and our work–life balance.

We need time to make memories. We need togetherness to make a relationship. Society tells us that this busy life is living the dream. But I beg to differ.

EMBRACING A COUNTERCULTURAL LIFE

When my husband and I had been dating for several years, I made it known to him that I didn't want a diamond engagement ring. Not that he was asking, but you know—I was a planner.

All of my friends had diamonds. Because "A Diamond is Forever." That means society tells you that if you can afford it, an engagement ring should be a diamond. *The bigger the better.* But who writes these rules anyways? Because I am not buying it. A diamond is in fact forever. You can treat it terribly, run it over with a car, and stomp on it. I promise you that it will remain completely intact and unchanged.

A diamond does not resemble a marriage. A marriage is a pearl. It's beautiful and unique, but it needs to be treated with respect because it can, in fact, be damaged. It can be marked. It can be destroyed.

So, I went for the pearl.

You don't have to strive for the biggest diamond. You don't have to seek the stuff. Your worth is far more than anything that you can buy.

The life I have proposed in this book is countercultural. That means I am proposing that you choose pearls over diamonds. I am proposing that you live intentionally and choose what matters most in your heart. When it comes to stuff, we need to carefully consider how we accumulate it. Then we need to do what aligns with our personal values and goals.

We need to do it for ourselves and for our children.

CHOOSE TO PARENT WITH LESS STUFF

By choosing to live with less stuff, you are trading chaos for calm. You are your child's first teacher; you are your child's biggest role model. You are making choices for your children that will impact their entire life in the years to come. It all starts with you.

Above all, be confident that living with less stuff will bring your children so much more.

Once you start living lighter with your family, you will never look back. Your friends may raise their eyebrows. You might not always have full approval from the in-laws. But follow your heart. *For your family, there's so much more hidden in less:*

1. Buy less.
2. Fear less.
3. Referee less.
4. Hurry less.
5. Entertain less.

In less you will find simple happy parenting.

HOW TO PARENT
WITH LESS STUFF

☐ FOCUS ON THE REAL GIFTS

The children of today are inundated with stuff. Much of this comes from well-intentioned loved ones. But the way we give also teaches our children. Therefore, it's important that we consider the quality, quantity, and frequency of stuff that we give to our children. When we give fewer tangible gifts, it's easier for our kids to focus on the real gifts of love and life.

☐ IT STARTS WITH YOU

The relationship that we have with stuff will impact the way our children relate to it as well. If you are looking to make a change and cut back on stuff, it's important to take a look at how your relationship with stuff works. Ask yourself how it was formed and how you can move forward to make intentional choices to live with less.

☐ EMBRACING A COUNTERCULTURAL LIFE

When you begin living with less stuff, you are moving in a way that runs counter to the norms of our present-day society. Expect that this path won't always be easy—you may find yourself taking two steps forward and one step back.

☐ CHOOSE TO PARENT WITH LESS STUFF

By choosing to live with less you are choosing a simpler, lighter life. You should feel confident that your children need less to be happy and thrive. There is so much more hidden in less, and once you start to peel back the layers you won't ever look back.

Mindful shopping

Tiny trinkets or toys rarely hurt our pocketbook and they bring brief surges of joy in our children. But there is more to the story. When we invite "stuff" into our home we need to give thought to the lifespan of the object.

We come into this world with nothing and we will leave this world with nothing. But much of the stuff that we own will be sticking around on Earth a lot longer than we will. That trinket will bring your son joy for eight minutes. And because it doesn't hold any financial or sentimental value it will end up dropped in a parking lot.

Just because an object leaves our possession doesn't mean it's gone. All of our trinkets have a lifespan. It looks like this:

1. The object is manufactured,

2. We acquire it,

3. We get rid of it,

4. It lives a long, empty, ownerless life in the landfill.

When we are buying, let's buy for the long haul. Let's buy things that we will value and keep. Let's buy things that can be reused, recycled, or will live long, full lives with other families after they leave our home.

Stop buying low-quality items that last a week and end up in the landfill. That means birthday party favors, dentist office treasure boxes, and vending machine treats. Our kids are watching us and studying the way we make decisions about buying and disposing. Let's lead by example.

You are not a mean parent, you are a responsible parent who is taking care of this planet. So please, stop buying disposable rubbish that will clutter your home and our planet.

Meet Zoë Kim

We are raising children in an era of disposability. Society tells us that children are frivolous. As a result, we feel the need to purchase excess clothes, toys, and food to keep up with the steady continuum of waste and consumption that they produce. But as families we can aspire toward wasting less. My good friend Zoë Kim is a supporter of the zero-waste movement. She and her four children reside in Atlanta, Georgia. Zoë is the founder of Raising Simple and the author of the book *Minimalism for Families*.

So, I asked Zoë...

How can families waste less?

Here's how she answered:

Raising a happy, healthy family whilst simultaneously minimizing waste can be overwhelming. The goal of wasting less can be easily buried by the sheer amount of clutter and activities that comes with raising kids. But I was determined to reduce my family's waste and teach my children to be better stewards—and that's what led me to zero waste.

There are a few definitions of zero waste. The simple one: Aim to send nothing to the landfill. Sounds impossible, right? Fortunately, there is a formula for families as coined by zero-waste pioneer Bea Johnson: the five Rs. Refuse what you do not need; reduce what you do need; reuse what you consume; recycle what you cannot refuse, reduce, or reuse; and rot (compost) the rest. Here are a few ways you can waste less with the five Rs:

Toys

There's a huge problem with kids' toys that no one's talking about—plastic toys, which account for 90 percent of the toy market are essentially destined for the landfill[2].

Actions:

- Start refusing things you don't need. When we hold onto stuff we don't need, we keep it from being useful to other people.
- It's time to significantly increase your standards for new toys coming into your home. Invest in quality open-ended toys. These are toys that typically have a longer play-life and can work for kids across different ages, gender, and interests. Reuse the gender-neutral quality toys with siblings and utilize your local thrift store!

Clothes

The average American throws away 70 pounds of clothing each year—and an overwhelming 85 percent of used clothing goes straight to landfill (3). Residents of the United Kingdom have nearly $50 billion of unused clothing hanging in their closets. When I buy clothes, I try to be a conscious consumer. I ask of each item: Was it made ethically, sustainably, and is it in my budget? By the way, the most environmentally friendly clothing option is wearing the clothes you already have.

Actions:
- Say "no" to fast fashion and impulse buys.
- Set time aside to do a full wardrobe edit of your kids' clothes. If you have items in great condition and want to recoup some cash, take them to a local thrift store, or try an online reseller. With new recycling resources and organizations popping up every year, it's best to research online or in your community.
- Reuse what you can and then shop your local thrift stores when items are needed. When you need to purchase new clothing for your kids, consider ethical clothing brands.

Food

Did you know that according to research by the United States Department of Agriculture, you're likely to waste more food than other households if you have young children at home? Planning, shopping, cooking, and feeding your family healthy meals is a source of stress for many parents. Add on the goal of sending nothing to the landfill and now we're overwhelmed wondering how to move forward.

Actions:
- Use those leftovers.
- Take a snack food waste challenge. Ask your kids to plan and eat a zero-waste snack for one week.
- Find a meal planning system that works for you. Planning ahead not only reduces waste, it also allows you to make fewer grocery trips, saving time and mental energy. Create a menu with three to five meals you can create

with leftover fruits and veggies. A few of my go-tos are vegetable and pasta soup, fried rice, roasted veggies, quiche, and fruit smoothies.

- Set boundaries for pre-meal snacking. This helps to keep our children's meal proportions consistent. If we pile too much on their plates, some of it is likely to go to waste.
- Refuse food in packaging that can't be recycled whenever possible. Shop with reusable fabric bags in your local loose bulk-food section. This allows you to purchase the exact quantity you need and reduce the chance it'll end up in the trash.
- Teach your kids about food. One way we have done this is to compost. We use a rotating bin to compost and the kids love the process, and the worms!

Whether your household produces ten bags or one jar of trash, with a little commitment and focus, working one or two actions from above will help make lasting changes in your family. Lessons learned early in childhood can prompt a lifetime of healthy habits, so let's help our kids become food-waste aware and conscious consumers.

ACKNOWLEDGMENTS

First and foremost, I would like to thank my husband David. He has been a tireless supporter of me, this book and my career. He took on the financial responsibility for our family as I worked through my doctoral degree and built a career. He is my greatest love and I am grateful every day that I get to do life with him.

I would also like to thank my children for their daily inspiration. They are my heart and soul and have been my greatest teachers.

I am thankful for my editor Philippa Wilkinson and her team at Quarto for coming to me with this book idea. Her support throughout the book writing process made it seamless and dare I say, almost "easy."

I am so pleased that Amy Drucker chose to photograph this book—her work has captured my heart in ways that I didn't know photography could. She worked diligently to capture amazing photos of small children who didn't always feel like having their photos taken. Amy has become a friend and I am grateful that she was my partner in this process.

I'd like to thank Manon de Jong for the beautiful illustrations she brought to the book. Her work is inspirational and really brought the "happy" feel to Simple Happy Parenting.

I feel fortunate that my friends Melissa Coleman, Erica Layne, Zoë Kim, Eloise Rickman, and Nicole Kavanaugh contributed to this book. Their wisdom has made this book more complete and it wouldn't have been the same without their words.

Lastly, I would like to thank the thousands of families across the world who have followed me on the journey I have been on with the Simple Families blog, podcast, and community. Your support has kept me going and inspired me more than you will ever know.

ENDNOTES

1. Dimensionality of Helicopter Parenting and Relations to Emotional, Decision-Making, and Academic Functioning in Emerging Adults http://journals.sagepub.com/doi/abs/10.1177/1073191116665907 ?journalCode=asma

2. https://www.nimh.nih.gov/health/statistics/any-anxiety-disorder.shtml

3. Persistent Fear and Anxiety Can Affect Young Children's Learning and Development https://developingchild.harvard.edu/wp-content/uploads/2010/05/Persistent-Fear-and-Anxiety-Can-Affect-Young-Childrens-Learning-and-Development.pdf

4. https://ajp.psychiatryonline.org/doi/10.1176/appi.ajp.2015.14070818

5. Eley TC, Collier D, McGuffin P, et al.: Anxiety and eating disorders, in Psychiatric Genetics and Genomics. Oxford, United Kingdom, Oxford University Press, 2002, pp 303–340 Google Scholar

6. https://ourworldindata.org/

7. Larson, R. W., & Almeida, D. M. (1999). Emotional transmission in the daily lives of families: A new paradigm for studying family process. DOI: 10.2307/353879

8. Middlebrooks, Jennifer S. and Audage, Natalie C. (2008) The Effects of Childhood Stress on Health Across the Lifespan. Project Report. National Center for Injury Prevention and Control of the Centers for Disease Control and Prevention.

9. Gray, Peter. (2011) The Decline of Play and the Rise of Psychopathology in Children and Adolescents. American Journal of Play

10. Jeanne E. Arnold, Anthony P. Graesch, Enzo Ragazzini, and Elinor Ochs. Life at Home in the 21st Century

11. Amber J. Hammons, Barbara H. Fiese. (2011) Is Frequency of Shared Family Meals Related to the Nutritional Health of Children and Adolescents? Pediatrics May 2011, peds.2010-1440; DOI: 10.1542/peds.2010-1440

12. Burdette HL, Whitaker RC. Resurrecting Free Play in Young ChildrenLooking Beyond Fitness and Fatness to Attention, Affiliation, and Affect. Arch Pediatr Adolesc Med. 2005;159(1):46–50. doi:10.1001/archpedi.159.1.46

13. Appold, Karen. "Time for bed? America's kids aren't getting enough sleep: the national sleep foundation's 2014 poll found that children are getting less-than-recommended sleep, but parents can play a powerful role in establishing good sleep habits for their kids." RT for Decision Makers in Respiratory Care, May 2014, p. 24+. Academic OneFile, Accessed 3 July 2018.

14. Hyson, Marilou. (2003) Putting early academics in their place. Educational Leadership, v60 n7 p20-23 Apr 2003

15. Dee TS, Sievertsen HH. The gift of time? School starting age and mental health. Health Econ. 2018; 27:781–802. https://doi.org/10.1002/hec.3638

16. Anna V. Fisher, Karrie E. Godwin, and Howard Seltman. (2014) Visual Environment, Attention Allocation, and Learning in Young Children: When Too Much of a Good Thing May Be Bad

17. Dauch, C., Imwalle, M., Ocasio, B., and Metz, A. (2018). The influence of the number of toys in the environment on toddlers' play. Infant Behavior and Development.https://doi.org/10.1016/j.infbeh.2017.11.005

18. Janssen, Ian (2015) Active Play as a Strategy for Preventing Childhood Obesity. Canadian Journal of Diabetes, Volume 39, S6

19. Williams, Lawrence (2014) The Heart of Learning. Oak Meadow Incorporated.

RESOURCES

Books

Slow: Simple Living in a Frantic World by Brooke McAlary

Minimalism for Families by Zoë Kim

Chasing Slow by Erin Loechner

The Minimalist Kitchen by Melissa Coleman

Clutterfree with Kids by Joshua Becker

Toddler Discipline for Every Age and Stage by Aubrey Hargis

Soulful Simplicity by Courtney Carver

The Minimalist Way by Erica Layne

The Whole Brain Child by Daniel Siegel and Tina Payne Bryson

You Are Your Child's First Teacher by Rahima Dancy

There's No Such Thing as Bad Weather by Linda Åkeson McGurk

Websites

www.simplefamilies.com

www.becomingminimalist.com

www.nosidebar.com

www.raisingsimple.com

www.ericalayne.co

www.janetlansbury.com

www.gottman.com

www.fridabemighty.com

www.thekavanaughreport.com

www.sprout-kids.com

www.childoftheredwoods.com

www.becomingunbusy.com

www.designformankind.com

www.alifeinprogress.ca

www.bemorewithless.com

www.betterpostpartum.com

Podcasts

Simple Families

Unruffled

The Slow Home Podcast

Optimal Daily Living

The Simple Show

The Minimalists

INDEX

INDEX

ABOUT THE AUTHOR

Denaye Barahona is the founder of Simple Families, a blog, podcast, and online learning community dedicated to helping families live well with young children. First and foremost, however, Denaye is a mother and wife. She and her husband started their family and adventure as parents in 2013 when they welcomed their son, and their daughter completed them in 2016.

Denaye has a personal and professional passion for helping women thrive in motherhood, with a Ph.D. in Child Development with a focus in Family Wellness. She is also a clinical social worker with a specialty in Child and Family Practice and has a Post-Grad Certificate in Behavior Analysis of Children. She has spent her career coaching parents and supporting families.

Denaye loves to travel [yes, with kids], talk all-things-health-and-food, and give preposterous amounts of unsolicited parenting advice. Whether it is from her on-the-job training as a mama or her professional experience, she has learned that as parents we so desperately want to get everything right, but in the process, we have the tendency to overcomplicate, overthink, and get overwhelmed.

Denaye is here to convince you that simple really is smart. She advocates taking a holistic approach to helping the whole family stay well: physical, emotional, and relational. That means living well by developing a healthy relationship with yourself, your family, and your home.

To learn more and join the Simple Families community, visit **simplefamilies.com**

ABOUT THE PHOTOGRAPHER AND ILLUSTRATOR

Amy Drucker is an award-winning photographer, teacher and author specializing in both lifestyle and documentary photography. Amy has worked with hundreds of families over the past fifteen years to document and tell their unique stories. Her work focuses on the intimate interactions between family members and on finding and immortalizing the beauty in everyday moments. She teaches photography classes and writes about the subject for multiple online and print outlets. Amy lives in the suburbs of New York City with her partner and their blended family: two sons and more cats than she wants to publicly admit.

Manon de Jong is an illustrator who is inspired by motherhood and the beauty in everyday moments. After studying philosophy and fashion design, she decided to turn illustration and graduated from the Hogeschool voor de Kunsten in Utrecht, the Netherlands in 2013. Her work mixes traditional and digital media, drawing elements with pencil, ink and marker and is combined through collage. Manon's illustrations have appeared in magazines including *Parents, Vogue Bambini, Flow* and *Natural Parent*. She lives in Amsterdam with her boyfriend and two young sons, Sam and Lucas.

Brimming with creative inspiration, how-to projects and useful information to enrich your everyday life, Quarto Knows is a favourite destination for those pursuing their interests and passions. Visit our site and dig deeper with our books into your area of interest: Quarto Creates, Quarto Cooks, Quarto Homes, Quarto Lives, Quarto Drives, Quarto Explores, Quarto Gifts, or Quarto Kids.

First published in 2019 by White Lion Publishing,
an imprint of The Quarto Group.
The Old Brewery, 6 Blundell Street
London, N7 9BH,
United Kingdom
T (0)20 7700 6700
www.QuartoKnows.com

Text © 2019 Denaye Barahona
Illustrations © 2019 Manon de Jong
Photographs © 2019 Amy Drucker

A catalogue record for this book is available from the British Library.

ISBN 978 1 78131 864 5
Ebook ISBN 978 1 78131 865 2

10 9 8 7 6 5 4 3 2 1

Design by Ginny Zeal

Printed in China